Louis W. Dawson II

10TH MOUNTAIN HUT & TRAIL SYSTEM

Colorado 10th Mountain Trails

OFFICIAL SKI TOURING GUIDE

WHO PRESS · ASPEN, COLORADO

DEDICATION

Dedicated to Billy Tagert, Alfred A. Braun,
and all those pioneer skiers who are long forgotten,
but on whose shoulders we stand.

PUBLISHED BY

WHO Press
410 Free Silver Ct.
Aspen, Colorado 81611

Library of Congress Catalog Card Number: 89-51652

ISBN 0-9620046-4-2

Printed in the United States of America

All photos by Lou Dawson unless otherwise indicated

Book design by Curt Carpenter

Foreword

As I go through this busy life, I relish my time in places of solitude and beauty. Such places provide a kind of meditation, an escape from the humdrum world. I like to call it "the icing on the cake of life." The 10th Mountain hut and trail system has given me many such experiences. A couple of years ago one of my compadres on such a trip looked at me after floating through waist-deep powder and commented, "With snow like this anyone can feel like a ski god." I agree.

My first experience with the 10th Mountain system was with my wife and parents. We began our trip in Aspen, skied east to the McNamara and Margy's huts, then out to the Diamond J Guest Ranch. Looking back, this three-day trip was one of the best times I have ever had with my parents. But it was also an epic. Even though we were all intermediate or advanced skiers, we had problems such as underestimating travel times, carrying too much equipment, and having the wrong ski gear for the downhill sections of trail. Since this first trip I've used the 10th Mountain system regularly. I've learned how to cope with most problems, but one has continued to plague me: a lack of information about the trails. As a result, I stick with familiar pastures and ignore new and exciting options.

I met Lou Dawson when he did some writing for us at *Rocky Mountain Sports and Fitness Magazine*. I was intrigued by the way he conveyed the excitement of backcountry travel while weaving good information on safety, navigation, and other factors into the fabric of his story. Recently, I met up with Lou in Telluride for some spring corn skiing on El Diente Peak. This was the first time I had skied with the man, and the trip was another memorable adventure. I was highly impressed by Lou's knowledge of backcountry skiing and his love for the sport. His reputation for being one of the finest ski mountaineers is well deserved.

Lou's previous guide *Colorado High Routes* covered some of the 10th Mountain huts and trails. However, the system has grown to the point where it needs a guide of its own, as shown by the book you hold in your hands. Speaking for myself, there will be no more skiing the trails over and over. As soon as I feel like something new, the information I need is right here, between these pages. Thus, I am ecstatic about *Colorado 10th Mountain Trails*. I'm certain that many other skiers will feel the same.

John Winsor
PUBLISHER, *Rocky Mountain Sports & Fitness*

ACKNOWLEDGMENTS

One person could never provide all the facts in a book such as *Colorado 10th Mountain Trails*. Scott Messina, who has set trails for 10th Mountain for several years, was an invaluable help. Thanks also to the staff at 10th Mountain for answering my endless questions. My wife Lisa deserves a special thanks for ignoring the long hours and weird schedule of a writer. And finally, I'd like to acknowledge my grandfather, L.W. Dawson, for his encouragement and support.

Thanks to the Skadi Corporation for the avalanche transceiver, and to Outdoor Research for sundry equipment. Kaestle and Dynastar supplied me with excellent skis, and thanks to Total Sports for the Dachstein DC ski boots. The Mountainsmith pack was terrific.

Berg Heil!

Preface

For many years the world over, mountain huts have sheltered skiers and climbers. In the Alps, hundreds of huts hang from mountainsides, and many have been in use for over a century. In the 1940s in Colorado, a chain of shelters cut through what is now the Maroon Bells-Snowmass Wilderness. The first ski hut in Colorado was created in the late 1940s, when Billy Tagert and his friends fixed up an old miner's cabin at the head of Castle Creek near Aspen. Tagert and his group loved ski mountaineering, but they knew that skiing with a load of camp gear could turn fun into plain toil.

Winter camping still makes for a pack that could break a mule, and you spend hours on pure survival, with skiing being the last item on your list. Ski huts relieve those burdens. Since those old timers skied Castle Creek, scores of ski shelters, ranging from primitive to palatial, have been built in Colorado.

The most extensive and popular of these ski hut systems is managed by the the 10th Mountain Trail Association (10th Mountain). A nonprofit corporation, 10th Mountain was formed in the early 1980s by several Aspen skiers who cherished the perfect ski touring between Vail and Aspen. From the beginning they set their sights on a trail with closely spaced shelters, all accessible via intermediate ski touring trails. The 10th Mountain name honors the soldiers of the 10th Mountain Division of the U.S. Army, who trained in the mountains between Aspen and Vail (see Appendix 2).

If there were a Hilton of backcountry skiing and lodging, 10th Mountain would qualify. In all, they book about 20 accommodations in the area bordered by Aspen, Vail, Leadville, and Crested Butte, Colorado. Eleven of these form a loop north and east of Aspen, through the vicinity of Vail and Leadville. This is known as the 10th Mountain hut and trail system, and is the system covered by this guide. For the area south of Aspen, 10th Mountain makes reservations for the Alfred A. Braun huts, Toklat Chalet, and the Friends Hut. Routes to these huts can be found in *Colorado High Routes*.

The 10th Mountain trails are approved by the Forest Service, and marked with blue plastic diamonds and tree blazes. As a convention in this book, these marked trails are called 10th Mountain suggested routes, as opposed to branch routes which explore terrain around the huts, and alternate routes which are simply routes that are not marked and Forest Service approved.

The 10th Mountain suggested routes are well marked and heavily traveled.

Thus, you'll find navigation to the huts is fairly easy, given good weather and a modicum of map work. Yet after a few trips from trailheads to huts, many skiers realize that perhaps the greatest benefit of the 10th Mountain system is the access it gives to alternate routes. This is especially true of travel in the designated wilderness bordered by many of the huts. The 10th Mountain suggested route is like an interstate highway, with country roads and turnoffs that are not always obvious.

This guide will help you use the 10th Mountain suggested routes — the "Interstate". It will give you essential information on trailhead access, parking, trip planning, and navigation. *Colorado 10th Mountain Trails* will also help you turn from the beaten path onto the country roads. Enjoy.

How To Use This Book

CHAPTERS

The chapters in this book are organized around the individual 10th Mountain backcountry huts. For example, if you want routes for travel from the Peter Estin Hut to the Polar Star Inn, turn to the Peter Estin Hut chapter; for the reverse turn to the Polar Star Inn chapter. A glance at the table of contents will clarify this.

TRAILHEADS

The trailhead is where you start your nonmotorized travel, and where you usually park. The trailheads are marked on all the maps. Directions to all the trailheads are given in Chapter 1.

Most trailheads are well signed, but signs change. Another concern is just where the snow closure is on access roads. This varies from year to year because of weather and plowing policy. For closure information you have two resources: the county's road maintenance division and the Forest Service. General information about snow closure is included in the text.

ROUTE INFORMATION

ROUTE NUMBER AND NAME: Each route is numbered with a conjunction of chapter number and the route's consecutive number within the chapter. For example, route 4.6 means Chapter 4, route 6. The routes are named using points of origin and destination. There are three kinds of routes in each chapter:

• Routes between trailhead and hut.

• Routes from hut to hut.

• Branch routes from the hut to a destination other than a hut or trailhead.

DIFFICULTY RATING: To help you pick routes that match your skills, all the routes are rated for novice, intermediate, advanced, or expert skiers. (See pp. 13-14 for description of each skill level.) Since the 10th Mountain suggested routes are designed as intermediate routes, you'll notice a majority of intermediate routes in the text.

TIME: The travel time is an estimate taken from an average of reported times. As such, it should only be used as a general guide. It assumes the trip was made by intermediate level skiers.

DISTANCE: Distances are one-way for trailhead — hut and hut to hut routes; they are round trip for all branch routes.

ELEVATION GAIN AND LOSS: The elevation gain and loss figures include most of the smaller ups and downs. In the trailhead—hut routes, the elevation change is given for the trailhead to hut direction. In the hut to hut routes, the change is given for the direction of travel. In the branch routes, the elevation changes are for the round trip.

MAPS: The USGS maps listed in the data block are the USGS 7.5 minute 1:24000 maps. These are best used as trail maps, but can double as road maps. The 10th Mountain maps are the same scale as the USGS maps and are marked with the 10th Mountain suggested routes. The 10th Mountain maps are composites of the USGS maps and are specifically designed for users of the hut and trail system. The area covered by the text maps corresponds to the area covered by the 10th Mountain maps. For the best road finding, use a Colorado road map and a USFS Forest Visitor map such as the White River National Forest map. The USFS maps are updated often, and cover large areas with a scale of ½ inch to a mile.

ROUTE DESCRIPTION: Route descriptions are given for both directions in the trailhead—hut routes. For the hut to hut routes, the descriptions start at the hut described in that chapter. The descriptions for the branch routes are for round-trip travel.

ATTENTION READERS

The information presented in this book is based upon the experience of the author and might not necessarily be perceived as accurate by other persons. Therefore, extreme care should be taken when following any of the routes described in this book. This book is not intended to be instructional in nature but rather a guide for skiers who already have the requisite training, experience and knowledge. An advanced level of expertise and physical conditioning is necessary for even the "easiest" of the routes described. Proper clothing and equipment is essential. Failure to have the necessary knowledge, equipment and conditioning will subject skiers to extreme physical danger, injury or death. Some routes have changed and others will change; avalanche hazards may have expanded or new hazards may have formed since this book's publication.

Table of Contents

The 10th Mountain Huts & Trails

The 10th Mountain Trail Association provides backcountry lodging for ski tourers, though certain lodging is available for summer use. Termed 'huts' in backcountry parlance, this lodging ranges from small cabins near timberline to lodges or inns that supply all the amenities from running water to catered meals. Reservations are required for all hut use.

Most of the huts in this book are owned by 10th Mountain, while some are privately owned. Several of the latter are booked by 10th Mountain, while others do their own booking. To make reservations at a hut, call 10th Mountain or the privately owned lodge or inn (see Directory). Most huts are booked well in advance, so plan ahead.

Users of this guide should remember that, though existing 10th Mountain owned lodging changes little from year to year, there can be drastic changes in privately owned lodging. Current information on all the huts is available through 10th Mountain.

Who Should Use the Huts and Trails

Now that huts can make camping unnecessary, skiers with less skill and vigor are enjoying the winter wilds. Even so, you still need a level of skill and strength to travel safely on the trails in this book, and you must know your limits. Weather can make any tour an epic, and illness, injury, or navigation problems can force you into a bivouac. The alternate and branch routes in this guide run the gamut of winter challenge and risk.

Sure, these trails travel to and from cozy shelters; but they are full-bore treks, not 'day trips'. You might have to break trail in deep powder and navigate in zero visibility conditions in the midst of a Rocky Mountain storm—all at altitudes over 8,000 feet. In short: no route in this book is an easy backcountry trail, there is no such thing. Thus, you should be at least an intermediate level backcountry skier to enjoy these trails on your own.

Though only several routes in this book are suitable for beginners, most novices will find plenty of enjoyable skiing in the region, mostly by skiing within a short distance of the various trailheads. The several routes that are rated novice should only be attempted by novice skiers accompanied by skiers with backcountry experience. Also, novice skiers can always hire a guide service to insure a safe, fun hut trip.

Intermediate, advanced, and expert backcountry trails require the following skill levels:

Intermediate backcountry skiers can use a strong snowplow for downhill control. They can change direction with a parallel or telemark turn, though they may not be highly skilled in downhill skiing. They have done long tours with at least 2,000 feet of elevation gain, at altitudes over 8,000 feet. Intermediates know how to read a topographic map, compass, and altimeter. They have plenty of first-aid knowledge, and carry and know how to use bivouac gear. Avalanche safety is more theory than experience for an intermediate, as they need field practice to learn hazard recognition.

Advanced backcountry skiers have all the skills of an intermediate, with the addition of several years experience skiing to the huts, and better ski skills. They usually have their first-aid card and are well versed in emergency conduct. Their orienteering skills are impeccable, and they have the fitness to ski for long days with over 3,000 vertical feet elevation gain. They have taken an avalanche safety course, and continue to study avalanche safety.

Expert backcountry skiers combine superb avalanche safety knowledge and climbing skills with their expert level skiing skills. They probably have at least eight years of solid experience, and have made the craft of wilderness skiing into an important hobby. Expert skiers are skilled enough to organize a rescue.

The spacious kitchen of the Fowler/Hilliard Hut

The Huts

Unlike many huts in Colorado, 10th Mountain's huts can sleep large numbers of people — usually 16 — and are often rented to several groups at a time. The whole hut can be rented for a flat fee.

Cooking is done by the hut users in communal kitchens. All the huts are stocked with eating and cooking utensils, and have gas burners. Most of the huts have no plumbing, so water is dipped or pumped from a spring, or melted from snow; the bathroom is an outhouse. The lodges and inns usually have plumbing and optional food service; many also supply full bedding. At the huts you'll find mattresses, but you'll have to bring your own sleeping bag. Since you'll be sleeping in a heated building, a lightweight sack will suffice. Pillows are available as well, so bring an oversized pillow case.

ETIQUETTE

In order to maintain the huts and the trails for everyone's enjoyment, a code of etiquette has been developed by 10th Mountain and the users. Civilized manners will help make the touring experience pleasant for all of the groups using the hut system. The following rules should always be observed.

Dogs are not allowed at the huts for several reasons. First, snow is melted for drinking water at many of the huts, and dogs contaminate the source snow. Second, dog tracks ruin packed trails, and skiing through dog feces is unpleasant at best. Finally, dogs harass wildlife. Hut crashers, people who stay a night at the hut with no reservations, will be prosecuted as trespassers.

It's also very important to be quiet in the evening when other users go to bed. Though 10th Mountain has no set quiet time, most county noise ordinances are in effect from around 10:30 P.M. to 7:00 A.M.: these are good guidelines for hut users.

There is no smoking allowed in the huts, both for fire safety and consideration of nonsmoking users.

At no time is drunkenness, wild partying, or rude behavior acceptable. The 10th Mountain roving hutkeepers have their eye out for abuses, as should all hut users.

PROCEDURES

HEATING: Most of the huts are heated by woodburning stoves. The wood is bucked, split, and stocked in the summer. Since wood gathering costs money and volunteer hours, conservation is important. First, keep the hut at a reasonable temperature — don't turn the place into a sauna. Second, study the outline for stove use that you'll find at the hut, and adjust the stove controls for an efficient burn. Finally, if the hut has a wood cookstove, and you use it, plan on extra cooking time; otherwise, you'll have to overstoke the stove to get enough heat.

Wood stoves are a fire hazard. For safety, the stove door should only be open while you're stoking or starting the fire. To build a fire, start with a small stack of paper and kindling, rather than a sloppy bonfire that can spill onto the floor or ignite the flue. Keep all inflammable material a good distance from the woodburner, including gear that you are drying. Many groups carry pack stoves for emergencies; keep these (and fuel) outside.

WATER: At many of the huts, you get water by melting snow on the woodburner. Several things can streamline this tedious chore. As soon as you get to the hut, light a fire. The snowmelt pot will be obvious; it's the biggest thing around, and is usually left on the stove. If the pot is empty take it outside, find some clean snow, and pack it densely. If the pot already has some water, leave it on the stove, and bring in the snow by shovel or plastic garbage bag. The key is to keep feeding snow to the pot while dipping out the melt. Finally, conserve water. Snow may look pure, but it's full of pollutants. It won't make you sick, but snowmelt can look and taste like three-day-old dishwater. Many skiers carry a filter pump for snow and stream water purification. Several huts have outside water sources. These are spring-sourced, and usually pure. If you have a sensitive stomach, you may still want to filter or treat the water.

COOKING: Cooking at the 10th Mountain huts is done in a communal kitchen. Thus, if there are several groups at the hut, they should stagger their kitchen work. Arranging this can test your diplomatic skills, but it will result in a nicer evening. It's a good idea to bring food with reasonable cooking time. Many a group has sat and grumbled while another took hours to create a multicourse feed worthy of the presidential dining room. Since wash water is scarce, plan meals that use a minimum of cookware.

You must carry out all your trash and uneaten food, so before you leave home, repackage foods that are in cans or jars. Eggs can be carried 'prescrambled' in a plastic bottle. In cold weather you can use tricks like carrying a frozen block of spaghetti sauce in a plastic bag. If you carry food that is only edible when cooked, be sure each person carries their own selection of trail food; you don't want to gnaw on frozen tomato sauce if you get separated from the group. Finally, plan your meals so that you don't haul extra food.

GENERAL HUT USE: If you're group is the last to leave the hut, you'll be the ones doing the sweeping and general cleanup. Other parties leaving earlier could keep things fair by stocking some wood or cleaning the toilets. There is always plenty to do.

The Trip

TRIP PLANNING

Backcountry skiing is complex. Food, gear, fitness, navigation, and group dynamics can overwhelm the best of us. Above all, keep it as simple as possible. Once you're in the field, you will regret lugging any more than the essentials. Grandiose route plans can sound good over cocktails at home, but you might have to set your sights lower if you're shooting for a fun, safe trip. Above all, remember that no book can make you an expert, but it can help you along the way. That's all *Colorado 10th Mountain Trails* will do. Put some thought into your travel style and transportation requirements. Most people leave from a trailhead, go to one hut, then return to the same trailhead. With some 'base skiing' from the hut, this kind of trip can be simple and fun. More experienced skiers can plan a 'ski-through' that connects two or more huts. On a one-way trip you will cover more new territory by not retracing your steps to your original starting point, but you will also have to arrange some kind of car shuttle. If you don't have friends in the area, or if it's inconvenient to perform your own shuttle, make arrangements — well in advance — with one of the shuttle services listed in the directory in the back of this book. It's usually most efficient to leave your car at the trailhead where you will be coming out, and have the shuttle take you and your party to the starting point of your trip.

TRAIL TECHNIQUE

Backcountry skiing is serious business. Ask some questions before you start. "Who's carrying the repair kit, the first aid kit? What if Joe's binding breaks and he's behind in Sherwood Forest?" To prevent that kind of situation, leave the trailhead as a group and travel within sight of each other. Drink every hour and eat light carbohydrates at least every two hours. Take short, regular rests every two hours. Avoid charging up the trail as if you're running the hundred-yard dash; the key is a slow, steady pace.

Dress lightly in layers and make extra stops to adjust your clothing. Even on a cold winter day, you can get heat exhaustion from overdressing. For travel in a snowstorm, wear thin undergarments under a full waterproof, breathable shell. Keep your hair dry by pulling the shell hood loosely over your head, or by wearing a shelled hat.

Most of the time you'll be following a packed trail. However, after a storm someone will have to break trail. Breaking out a ski trail is one of the most arduous tasks in mountain skiing. To make trail breaking easier, change the lead often and keep a steady — albeit slow — pace. Even on the flats, skins really help the 'break-out'. On packed trails, use climbing skins for uphills, but take the time to remove them for all but the shortest downhills.

TRAIL MARKERS

While many fine routes lead to, from, and around the 10th Mountain lodging, only certain trails are designated by the Forest Service as 10th Mountain suggested routes. These routes are marked with 5-inch x 7-inch high blue plastic diamonds nailed to trees, or with blazes hacked into tree bark when laws preclude hanging plastic in designated wilderness. Some direction changes are indicated by blue plastic arrows. This guide covers the marked routes, as well as unmarked alternate and branch routes.

Trail markers can become a follow-the-dots system for people who lack the skill to ski safely. Markers are difficult to place above timberline and in clearings; this can lead to confusion for skiers who expect frequent markers. Most veteran 10th Mountain skiers agree that to enjoy the trail, ignore markers and navigate from your maps. You should be saying, "Ah, another marker, we must have read our map right," rather than, "Hey, I can't find a diamond, did you bring a map?"

SAFETY

Avalanche danger is the most well-known risk in backcountry skiing. Fortunately, snowslide danger is minimal — or nonexistent — on the 10th Mountain suggested routes. Yet skiers who venture from the beaten path are sure to encounter slide terrain. Once buried by an avalanche, you have less than a a 50 percent chance of survival up to the first half hour, and no chance after that. Even if the slide does not bury you, just the savage ride down a mountain is likely to kill you.

The most important part of avalanche safety is hazard recognition. You can easily identify slopes where snowslides are possible: basically, any treeless or sparsely timbered slope steeper than 25 degrees. By learning about snowslides, you can practice hazard recognition and avoidance, and safely travel through moderate avalanche terrain. Formal training through avalanche school is a good place to start learning. To supplement your schooling, use weather reports and local avalanche hazard forecasts. Speak with local mountaineers about current conditions. Finally, go out and practice. One rule bears constant emphasis: EXPOSE ONE PERSON AT A TIME TO HAZARD. You do this by traveling one at a time through exposed areas, or by spreading your group out on routes that have repeated exposure.

Avalanche danger varies with the season. Midwinter in Colorado is always very dangerous, but there is usually an eight to twelve week corn snow season in the spring when danger is minimal and predictable. The spring season is the time to enjoy ski runs off the high peaks. To be safe, you have to get up early and ski before the late morning thaw. The 10th Mountain huts are closed during most of the alpine corn snow season, but if you're lucky, you can catch a few days of 'hut corn' towards the end of April.

Though avalanches are a bewitching hazard, illness and ski falls account for the most lost days and rescues on the routes in this book. At the altitude of the Colorado Plateau, you have about half the oxygen and humidity you get at sea level. For visitors from sea level, these changes can cause sickness and even death. The only sure way to prevent altitude sickness is by acclimating in steps. If you come from sea level, get to Colorado 48 hours before a hut trip. If you cannot schedule those extra days, try to spend your first hut nights at some of the lower-elevation huts, such as the McNamara Hut, Diamond J Guest Ranch, Rocky Mountain Health Ranch, or Harry Gates Hut.

If you must go high without acclimation, stay hydrated and don't exhaust yourself. Eat more carbohydrates for several days before you leave. Lower your salt intake and take iron pills. Above all, don't drink alcohol; it amplifies the effect of altitude. If you must have beer and wine, use low alcohol brands.

If you're acclimated and fit, but still feel awful (headache and malaise) after a day on the trail, chances are you're dehydrated. In one day of ski touring, you can loose more than a gallon of water from sweating, breathing dry air, and the diuretic effect of the cold. In addition, coffee and alcohol are diuretics. There are several ways to reduce dehydration. To begin with, limit your morning coffee to one cup, and tank up on water before you hit the trail. Then, since humans are not camels, stop and drink several ounces of water at least once an hour. Try some of the athletic drink mixes that can be added to your water. These are quickly absorbed and supply some calories. Another trick is to put a quarter of a lemon in your water bottle. This will flavor fill-ups for about a week.

No matter how careful most people are, they will probably be slightly dehydrated when they arrive at the hut. Thus, it is critical to drink as you step in the door. All this begs the question: how do you know you are hydrated? The answer is crude but effective: the more yellow the snow, the more water you should drink.

IF YOU GET INTO TROUBLE • *An Emergency Checklist*

The mountains are a dangerous place for us fragile humans, and no matter how careful we are, human error can strike. Thus, you should always be ready to handle your or someone else's emergency. To do so, you should be skilled in first and secondary aid, as well as moving an injured person over snow. Gain these skills by taking first-aid courses and studying books.

In Colorado, all search and rescue is done by expert teams under the direction of the county sheriff. Organized rescue groups aside, you must remember that an expedient rescue begins in the field with the victim and their party. Follow these guidelines:

Avalanche Rescue Drill

Before you leave on a trip, be sure someone in civilization knows of your route and schedule. This person should notify the county sheriff if you are overdue. Even with this arrangement, you will not get immediate help. Thus, you must handle things yourself.

In the case of an accident or illness, your first step in the field is to give the proper first aid. Next, move the person to a hut or bivouac. If you decide you need a rescue, send someone out for help. In a party of two, the victim will have to be left alone.

The person who goes for help should have a USGS map clearly marked with the location of the victim. He should ski with care to the nearest phone. To initiate the rescue, it's necessary to call the sheriff of the county in which the victim is located.

If the sheriff decides you need a rescue, he may authorize a helicopter. It is a good idea to bivouac as close as you can to a likely landing site. Mark your location with a large figure stamped in the snow. An SOS or an arrow pointing to your exact location will do fine. A smoky fire can help by acting as a signal and showing wind direction. Anchor all your gear to withstand the hurricane winds of helicopter rotors. If you haven't had time to construct good markers you'll have to signal the aircraft with your body. To do so, wear bright clothing, lay down in an open area, and wave your arms. Before nearing an operating helicopter, secure all your loose clothing, and carry skis at hip level horizontal to the ground.

EQUIPMENT

Gear—it's perplexing, expensive, and critical. Even after hours of shop clerk advice, and research worthy of a Greek scholar, many skiers still wonder exactly what equipment to use on the 10th Mountain trails. The problem is twofold: myriad choices, and trips that vary from the basic ones to mountain climbs on 13,000-foot peaks. The tips below will help you sort out the choices.

SKIS: 'Free-heel' gear refers to the 'three-pin' skis, boots and bindings used by most skiers on the routes in this guide. Alpine touring (AT) gear means wider alpine style skis, plastic boots, and bindings with an optional heel latch.

Unlike many ski huts in the Alps, Canada, and other countries, the 10th Mountain huts can be reached via long, relatively flat trails. So, though downhill skiing is harder on free-heel gear than with AT gear, most people on the 10th Mountain suggested routes use free-heel ski gear.

AT gear, even though it is less efficient on the flats, is used by many who venture higher into the mountains beyond the huts. Also, many people have found that an AT setup helps with the 'toboggan run downhills' on many of the hut to trailhead routes. Elderly skiers, for whom the consequences of a fall can be more severe, have found this to be especially true.

When picking out free-heel skis, consider your main use. If you stick to the 10th Mountain suggested trails, use the slightly lighter weight 'trail' models. If like to break out the alternate routes or go for powder skiing, you may want a wider, heavier ski. In either case, be certain that you use true backcountry free-heel skis, with steel edges, and at least 55 mm wide under the foot. By all means, do not use cross country track skis. AT skis are easier to pick; they are all wide enough and plenty strong. Choose them by the type of snow the skis are designed for—usually soft snow on the 10th Mountain routes. As for length, shorter skis, both AT and free-heel, save weight and can be carried on your pack without catching your partners chin or nipping your calves. But make sure your ski length is compatible with your weight while carrying a pack. Flex is a good clue to ski performance. As a rule of thumb, a softer flex will turn more easily in soft snow, while a stiffer flex gives you better edge hold on hard snow. Above all, weight is the enemy: you'll realize that every time you drag a ski through a stride. At least one equipment expert, when asked about the best and least expensive way to save weight, has pinched his paunch and smiled. Stay fit.

FOOTWEAR: As with skis, choosing touring boots can bemuse anyone. For touring on the 10th Mountain suggested routes, a medium weight free-heel boot will work well. But if your plans include ventures off the beaten path, look at boots that are designed with downhill turns in mind. If you plan on plan on winter camping, or have the slightest problem with cold feet, buy double boots. While in the shop, be sure you can put on your double boot shells while you're wearing the inners. That's because the inners make nice hut slippers, or during a bivouac—it happens—you may want to sleep with them on. Single boots cost less, and some people say they're better for the downhill skiing. However, they have more tendency to blister, and are just not as comfortable as doubles. For distance touring, lean toward softer, lighter boots, but don't use track racing boots.

What do you look for in an AT boot? For long tours, use lighter, softer boots. Experts who ski steep, spring corn snow like stiffer boots, but these usually compromise touring comfort. With all boots comfort is crucial. Too short, and they'll bruise and freeze your toes; too long, and they'll pinch and bind. Poor fit, combined with lack of blister prevention on the trail, can make your feet into hamburger. Start the boot-fit trail with buying your boots from a reputable shop. Boots by mail can be a disaster.

For boot accessories, super gaiters will do more to preserve your feet and boots than any other add-on. All super gaiters have one problem: boot attachment. The ones with a rubber rand are hard to fit, tend to pop off at the worst times, and if left on can ruin your boots by trapping moisture. Also the rubber instep yoke on these gaiters wears out quickly while boulder hopping or scree slogging. To get around these problems, many savvy trekers take the classic supergaiter—the one with nylon rather than rubber around the bottom—and simply screw the bottom edge of the gaiter to the boot welt with brass screws.

SKI BINDINGS: Free-heel bindings are simple. They come in two varieties: those with three pins that insert into your boot sole, and those with a cable that latches around your boot heel. The latter weigh more, but they give more control, and help your boots last longer. Since free-heel bindings cost so much less than other parts of a ski setup, and since they are so lightweight, simply buy the most durable ones you can find.

AT bindings differ from free-heel bindings in the complexity that allows them to perform in two different modes. They provide a solid, yet releasable attachment of boot to ski for downhill skiing, as well as a walking mode that allows the heel to move up and down. For the routes in *Colorado 10th Mountain Trails*, choose AT bindings that are light and allow full freedom of movement for walking. Some bindings limit how high you can heel lift. Also, use bindings that allow you to change modes without removing them from your feet. That way, you can latch your heels for short, scary downhills.

You can get good accessories for free-heel bindings. The *Voilé Plate* preserves your boots and enhances downhill performance. Another good option is the *Televate*, which lifts your heels for climbing. All AT bindings allow the use of ski crampons. These are a godsend for steep traverses or steep climbing. At least one version of ski crampons is made for free-heel skis.

SKI POLES: Every backcountry skier should have ski poles that convert to an avalanche probe. Even if you stay away from slide danger, you never know when a nearby accident will require your help. In addition to avalanche-probe capability, you have a choice of adjustable length or fixed length poles. Adjustable poles are good because they can be elongated for skating or diagonal striding, then shortened for downhill skiing. Adjustables are expensive, however, and they can be difficult to adjust in cold weather. Fixed length poles save a little weight, cost less, and are more reliable.

Pole straps should be made of wide nylon webbing, and be easy to adjust with gloves. A larger basket is nice for powder snow. The snowflake plastic design is the best; it is designed not to snag on vegetation and such. Large powder rings are helpful for long slogs, but avoid these if you do much downhill skiing. They snag, add weight, and are tough to pull up out of the snow after a pole plant.

CLIMBING SKINS AND WAX: Climbing skins are useful — perhaps essential — for the 10th Mountain suggested routes. They are a must for all alternate and branch routes. Skins were invented long ago when a clever Nordic skier strapped animal pelts to the bottom of his skis for traction. If the natural lay of the fur was aligned with the ski, with the hair ends pointed back, the skins would slide forward yet provide traction by virtue of the hairs penetrating the snow. These evolved into modern strap-on skins. Now most skiers use strapless 'stick-ons' that glue to the ski bottoms with special adhesive. Stick-on skins are terrific. They go on and off quickly, glide better, and weigh less. Moreover, they prevent ice chunks from forming between skin and ski, and give better edge hold on icy hillsides.

Occasionally, stick-ons don't stick. Hooking the skin on the ski tip and just wrapping the end of the skin up over the ski tail is an invitation to disaster. Duct tape may work for a few miles, but it will likely end up as unsightly trail litter. The solution is a tip and tail fix system. Also, refresh your glue often. Excellent products are available for doing this on the fly, but nothing refreshes like a fresh coat. When the temperature is below freezing, damp glue will freeze and not stick; take care while removing your skins to keep the glue dry, and consider keeping them warm under your jacket until the next application. The best way to protect the glue is to double each skin over and stick it to itself when it's not on the ski.

Climbing skins are available with three types of 'fur': a white nylon, a stiffer red or blue nylon, and black mohair (real goat hair). Nylon skins climb better and are less likely to form ice, but have poor glide. Mohair skins are not as durable, but weigh less and have better glide. Because most trails in the 10th Mountain region involve long distance travel on relatively low-angled terrain, mohair is the best choice.

As a general rule, use the widest skins you can without covering your edges. If you cover up your edges you won't be able to sidestep or snowplow. Skinny skins, though they glide well, require perfect technique for steep climbing.

Skins can be overkill on flat trails, and they take all control out of downhilling, though you can put them on backwards for "walking wounded" downhilling. For flat routes use Nordic wax. Any of the two-wax systems available will work fine. Apply wax in a thin layer so that it will be easy to remove before you put your skins back on.

PACKS: You can lump packs for hut skiing into two size categories. The smaller variety has little volume, a minimal internal frame or no frame at all. Medium sized packs have around 3,000 cubic inches volume and an internal frame. Small packs will work for an overnight hut trip—given minimal gear and some sacrifice of comfort or vino. On the other hand, if your ski adventures require survival gear, a shovel, winter clothing, and camera gear, you should use a medium size pack.

Many trailheads, peak ascents, and dry sections on the trails require walking. Thus, some sort of ski attachment is a vital pack feature. Ski slots behind pockets work, as do compression straps, but both these take time to rig. Lashing skis lengthwise, over or under the top flap, is favored by some people, especially those with shorter skis. Still another method is to put the ski tails down through the ice axe loops (many modern packs have two), then lash the upper portion of the skis to the pack. This works well because it angles the ski tails away from your legs.

Attaching a shovel to the pack can frustrate the most jolly mountaineer. Several packs are available with shovel holders, and are worth considering. If your pack does not have a dedicated shovel attachment, use extra lashing straps. Take care that the shovel blade will not hit you in the head if you fall, and be sure you can get it off quickly for avalanche rescue or sculpting a picnic table.

SHOVEL: Your shovel is as important as your clothing. It's mandatory for shelter building, avalanche rescue, and avalanche safety evaluation. A shovel can also serve as a stove platform, snow melter, or even part of a rescue sled. You have two choices in shovel materials: plastic and aluminum. Plastic is slightly lighter, and can bend repeatedly without breaking. Forces strong enough to bend aluminum will quickly break it, but it cuts better through hard snow such as frozen avalanche debris.

A telescoping shovel shaft is nice but not essential. Be sure the shovel grip fits your mittened hands. The grip should have a lashing hole; this is handy for everything from lashing to your pack to improvising a sled.

AVALANCHE RESCUE GEAR: Though most 10th Mountain suggested routes avoid avalanche danger, many groups venture into avalanche terrain while using alternate routes, or base skiing from a hut. Without the help of an electronic rescue beacon, recovering a person alive from an avalanche burial is like a blind man finding a friend at a rock concert. In avalanche terrain, each party member must carry, and know how to use, an avalanche rescue beacon, compact shovel, and convertible probe ski poles.

NAVIGATION AIDS: Map, compass and altimeter are the essentials for quality navigation. Though many intermediate skiers are unfamiliar with the altimeter, this simple device has been in use by mountaineers the world over for many years and is considered indispensable for safe, sure route finding in mountain terrain. Elevations are given in this book throughout all the route descriptions to aid your navigation. Avoid budget altimeters: they don't have the accuracy required for the backcountry.

The maps in this book are adequate for navigation on the 10th Mountain suggested routes, and are helpful for the alternate and branch routes. The 10th Mountain Trail Association sells larger scale topographic maps with the 10th Mountain suggested routes marked on them. If you plan on much exploring, or just want to get a broader view of things, you can also purchase USGS 7.5 minute topographic maps. These are available in local mountaineering stores, or by mail from the USGS.

The best compass is the kind with a clear plastic base and a dial that rotates on top of the base.

FIRST-AID KIT: In truth, few things you can carry in your first-aid kit will help with major medical problems. Indeed, the crucial items in this category are things such as sleeping bags, shovels, food, and some way of melting snow and heating water. Nonetheless, your kit should have supplies for splinting (such as some cravat bandages), one large-sized ace elastic wrap, and extra lash straps. For dressing wounds, bring athletic tape and some larger *Telfa* pads that you can cut to size. Include an antiseptic ointment and a small unbreakable bottle of *Betadine* soap.

More often than not, blisters are why you will dig into your kit. But don't wait until you are limping: the prevention of blisters is the key to a good trip. For starters, everyone but those with the toughest feet and broken-in boots should pretape their heels. To do this, simply swab the bony rear point of the heel with tincture of benzoin, tape vertically for three inches or more with athletic tape, dust the area with talc powder, then roll the sock on with care so the tape stays on. Some people like to use duct tape for this, but duct tape can cause skin reactions, so only use it if you've tested it on your skin. Though pretaping helps, it is of limited value because blisters are caused by pressure as well as rubbing. Thus, many people will feel 'hot spots' even after pretaping.

As soon as you get a 'hot spot', remove your boot and sock and stick a thick moleskin donut around the spot. Do not remove the old tape, just attach the donut with more athletic tape. The idea is to leave the tender "preblister" skin intact under the first layer of tape. If the moleskin is cold, warm the glue with a lighter for better adhesion. So: for blisters, add benzoin, talc, and moleskin to your kit. Some people like *Spenco Second Skin*; this should only be used for blister repair, not prevention, as its thickness causes more pressure.

Medication supplies are simple. For minor discomforts, bring antacid and a pain killer. A small bottle of artificial tears to treat dry-eye or wash out the eye is also handy. Everyone should carry a good sun block — at least SPF 15 — and use it.

WATER CONTAINER: Hydration is so crucial in the mountains that the the lowly canteen takes on a new meaning. Wide-mouth plastic bottles make the best water jars. Those available usually hold about a quart, so carry two if you plan on long days. Frozen water can be an acute problem during the colder winter months: sucking on a block of ice is no way to stay hydrated. To keep your water from freezing, fill your bottle up in the morning with hot water or tea, and wrap the bottle in extra clothing. Some people carry an unbreakable thermos, or one of the insulated jars available in mountaineering stores. The latter will cool sooner than a real thermos, but they never freeze.

HUT TRIP REPAIR KIT • *One Per Party*: Even the best equipment can fail, so carry a repair kit consisting of the following in a separate sack:

- Two three-pin bindings drilled with extra screw holes (you don't need a pair because left and right are interchangeable in a pinch).
- Extra oversize and regular-size binding screws, epoxy, and steel wool.
- Screwdriver for your binding screws — usually posidrive #3.
- Duct tape for taping your boot to your ski, or just about anything to anything else.
- Pliers with built-in wire cutter.
- Three yards malleable wire, like bailing wire.
- Two ski pole baskets.
- Three hose clamps for splicing broken poles.
- Thread, needle, and a few safety pins.
- Some strong nylon cord.
- Other repair items, as for stove repair.

CLOTHING: Bring clothing that's light, comfortable, and warm, even when damp. This rules out cotton; the new synthetic fabrics are a good choice, but wool still works well. Many people forget that very wet snow and rain are both possible during a Colorado winter, so your shell garments should keep out the wet, as well as the wind. The key to winter comfort is layering your clothes. Bring the following:

- Medium-weight long-underwear top and bottom for a foundation layer.
- Stretch tights for fair-weather or to double as a foundation layer.
- Breathable nylon windshirt for a fair-weather outer layer.
- Pile jacket and side-zip pile pants for main insulation layer (these pants are also good for hut lounging).
- An additional upper layer in midwinter.
- Side-zip wind pants and a good shell jacket made with one of the breathable coatings like Gore-tex for a bad-weather outer layer.
- Gloves with wrist gauntlets for colder weather and lightweight synthetic gloves for warmer conditions.
- A thick pile hat, a neck gaiter, wool or polypro socks, and a good pair of boot gaiters.

10th Mountain

Eagle
To Grand Junction

The Tenth Mountain Trail & Hut System
is located in the White River and San Isabel National Forests
and is under agreement with the Forest Service, USDA

8,220'

Polar Star
Inn
11,040'

9,060'   6.5 MILES
                              9,440'

8,558'

Peter Estin
Hut
11,200'

9.5 MILES
10.7 MILES
9,995'

New York Mtn
4

SAWATCH

9,180'

Harry Gates
Hut
9,700'

8,440'

To Basalt

Diamond J
Guest Ranch
8,250'

8,320'
Burnt Mountain 3
8,440'

Rocky Mountain
Health Ranch
8,760'

Margy's Hut
11,300'

Mount Yeckel
2

8,640'   9,450'

McNamara
Hut
10,360'

Aspen
8,380'

HUNTER FRYINGPAN WILDER

Bald Knob 1

x Trail System

8,220' **Vail**

Dowds Junction

Vail

[24]

[70]

Minturn

MINTURN

Shrine Mountain Inn 11,209'

Black Lakes

9.3 MILES

2.7 MILES

Vail Pass

10,610'

TE RIVER
NAL FOREST

8,680'

10.5 MILES

Pilgrim's Inn

6.8 MILES

10,820'

To Denver

SS WILDERNESS

Fowler/ Hilliard Hut 11,500'

6.8 MILES

2.8 MILES

6.4 MILES

9,678'

Resolution Mountain 5

Pando
9,200'

6.5 MILES

Schuss/ Zesiger Hut 11,660'

Camp Hale
9,250'

4.7 MILES

6.8 MILES

9,280'

9,580'

8.5 MILES

Vance's Cabin 10,980'

10th Mountain Division Hut 11,370'

13203

Tennessee Pass

3.7 MILES

5.7 MILES

10,424' Ski Cooper

Chicago Ridge 6

4.4 MILES

10,137'

Missouri Hill

SAN ISABEL NATIONAL FOREST

[24]

7.3 MILES

8.5 MILES

10,740'

11,680'

[91]

Uncle Bud's Hut 11,380'

5.8 MILES

9,880'

Galena Mountain 7

Leadville

MT. MASSIVE
WILDERNESS

Hut	▲	Trail
Trailhead	▲	Wilderness Boundary
Ski Area	✗	

0 1 2 3 4 5
SCALE IN MILES

The maps, roads and trails herein are general directions of
the areas only, and should not be relied upon for accuracy.

Entire Contents © 1989 Tenth Mountain Trail Association

29

Chapter 1 • Trailheads

The trailheads are arranged by region (highway or drainage), clockwise from Aspen. Finding the trailhead can be the most frustrating and time-consuming part of a backcountry trip, so follow the directions carefully and take your time.

Aspen Area

Hunter Creek Trailhead

ELEVATION: 8,380 feet
10TH MTN MAP: Bald Knob
USGS MAP: Aspen

To reach the Hunter Creek Trailhead, start in Aspen. Follow Main Street in Aspen to Mill Street (the stoplight next to the Hotel Jerome). Turn N on Mill and drive a short way down a hill, then across a bridge over the Roaring Fork River (.25 mile). Bear left after the bridge and follow the Red Mountain Road 1.2 miles to its second switchback. Just before the switchback, turn right and downhill onto the Hunter Creek Road. Drive .25 miles on Hunter Creek Road, then take a hard left on an unpaved driveway that leads up past a water tank several hundred feet to a parking area. The actual trailhead is farther up the mountain, but this is the only parking.

You have several choices for foot travel to the actual trailhead. The simplest method is to walk back down the driveway to the Hunter Creek Road, turn left through two stone gate posts that are marked Private, and follow the paved Hunter Creek Road ⅓ mile around a hairpin switchback to the well-signed Hunter Creek Trailhead on the right side of the road. Your other choice for foot travel is to follow a poorly marked foot trail that traverses up the mountain from the parking area to the trailhead. Perhaps the best way to deal with this trailhead is to enlist the services of a friend or taxi, and get dropped off at the actual trailhead.

Lenado Trailhead

ELEVATION: 8,640 feet
10TH MTN MAP: Bald Knob
USGS MAP: Aspen

From Aspen, drive 6 miles northwest on Highway 82. At the sign for Woody Creek Canyon, turn right and follow Smith Way .35 miles down a steep hill and across the bridge over the Roaring Fork River. At the T intersection just past the bridge, turn left and follow the Upper River Road 1.6 miles downvalley to a hard right onto the Woody Creek Road (sometimes called the Lenado Road). Drive the Woody Creek Road 8 miles to Lenado, a small group of rustic homes, then continue a short distance to the plow turnaround for the winter trailhead.

The Woody Creek Road begins as a paved road, then soon becomes a narrow unpaved track. It is fine for 2-wheel drive in good conditions, but it is one of the last roads the county plows and can have some mighty slick mud, so beware after storms. In the summer you can drive on the road past the winter closure. It switchbacks about 5 miles to 10,910 feet, just below the summit of Larkspur Mountain. This is a good starting place for hikes and mountain bike rides.

Lenado Alternate Trailhead

ELEVATION: 8,540 feet
10TH MTN MAP: Bald Knob
USGS MAP: Aspen

This trailhead is used for the Lenado Gulch route (2.3) from Lenado to the McNamara Hut. It is a hard trailhead to find; trailhead signs often disappear after a few weeks. The Forest Service has installed a few "no motor vehicle" stakes which may be there when you arrive, but don't count on it.

The best way to locate the trailhead is to use an odometer reading. The trailhead is located on the right side of the Woody Creek Road, exactly 8.2 miles from the Upper River Road. Of course, not all odometers are equal, so following is a verbal description: Follow the Woody Creek Road 8 miles to Lenado (see Lenado Trailhead description). Cross a bridge, drive a short way up a hill, then though the center of town (just a few buildings on both sides of the road) and look for the first telephone pole on the left as soon as you pass the buildings. The trail starts exactly across the road from this telephone pole.

Fryingpan Drainage

NOTE: *Fryingpan drainage trailheads are all located on or near the Fryingpan Road. To reach the Fryingpan Road, drive Highway 82 to Basalt from Aspen or Glenwood Springs. Drive E through Basalt on Midland Avenue (the main street), which soon becomes the Fryingpan Road (county road 104). All mileages below are measured from the Alpine Bank on Midland Avenue.*

Spring Creek Trailhead

ELEVATION: 8,440 feet
10TH MTN MAPS: Mount Yeckel, Burnt Mountain
USGS MAP: Meredith

Follow the Fryingpan Road 25.2 miles from Basalt to the well-signed Eagle Road on the left (N). Turn off the Fryingpan Road onto the Eagle Road and follow it 2.7 miles to the plow turnaround at the Spring Creek Fish Hatchery. Parking here can be tricky, as you must allow for the plow and autos to turn around. The best way to do this is to park well to the side of the road a short ways back down the road from the turnaround. The Eagle Road is well maintained, but think twice about driving with 2-wheel drive if you get there before the county plow.

In the summer, you can continue with 2-wheel drive all the way to Eagle. One caveat: do not attempt this road when it is wet—even with 4-wheel drive. Add a little rain or snow-melt and it becomes slicker than axle grease.

Diamond J Guest Ranch Trailhead

ELEVATION: 8,250 feet
10TH MTN MAPS: Mount Yeckel, Burnt Mountain
USGS MAP: Meredith

From Basalt, follow the Fryingpan Road 26.1 miles to the Diamond J Guest Ranch on the right (S) side of the road. Turn up the driveway, go over the bridge and up a short steep hill to the ranch parking area. Be sure to check at the lodge as to the best place to leave your vehicle. The trail heads SE from the main lodge through the cabin area. This trailhead is generally used by ranch guests; other skiers might find it more convenient to start at Norrie Trailhead or Mountain Haven Trailhead.

Mountain Haven Trailhead

ELEVATION: 8,320 feet
10TH MTN MAPS: Mt. Yeckel, Burnt Mt.
USGS MAP: Meredith

From Basalt, follow the Fryingpan
Road 26.1 miles to the Diamond J Guest
Ranch on the right (S) side of the road.
You might need to park here (see
below). For the Mountain Haven Trailhead, continue up the Fryingpan
Road .4 miles to a Y fork in the road (this area is known as Biglow). There
is a sign here that says Mountain Haven, and there may be a 10th Mountain trailhead sign. Take the left fork, then immediately turn up the first
driveway to the left (N) and follow a log fence to a gate across the road.
Look for the 10th Mountain blue diamonds. This gate is where you begin
skiing, though on lean snow years (especially in the spring) you might walk
up the road for several hundred more yards. Parking at this trailhead
depends on the whims of the snowplow and local landowners. For more updated parking information, ask for advice at the Diamond J Guest Ranch
or call 10th Mountain.

Norrie Trailhead

ELEVATION: 8,440 feet
10TH MTN MAP: Mount Yeckel
USGS MAP: Meredith

From Basalt, drive the Fryingpan Road 26.1 miles to the Diamond J Guest
Ranch on the right (S) side of the road. The ranch is well signed and easy
to spot. To drive to the Norrie Trailhead, continue up the Fryingpan Road,
staying right at the Biglow fork (see Mountain Haven Trailhead description). At 1.5 miles from the Diamond J Guest Ranch, take an obvious right
turn off the main road and drive several hundred feet to snow closure. This
turn is marked by a Norrie Colony sign and a Forest Service road sign 504.

There is little parking at this trailhead, so most people park at the
Diamond J Guest Ranch and either ski, walk, or car-shuttle to the Norrie
Trailhead. There is a well-defined ski trail on the south side of the valley
from the Diamond J to the Norrie Trailhead.

Rocky Mountain Health Ranch Trailhead

ELEVATION: 8,760 feet
10TH MTN MAP: Mount Yeckel
USGS MAP: Nast

This privately owned accommodation is located on 10th Mountain suggested routes that connect with Uncle Bud's Hut and Margy's Hut. It is also accessible by an all-season road, so it is treated here as a trailhead.

From Basalt, drive the Fryingpan Road 26.5 miles to the Biglow fork (by the Mountain Haven Trailhead). Take the right (S) fork and continue up the main paved road 5 miles to a well-signed right (S) turn-off. There is a sign here for Rocky Mountain Health Ranch (formerly the Horseshoe Bend Ranch), as well as one for Nast Lake and Granite Lakes Trailhead. After the turn-off, a winding dirt road leads 1.1 miles to the obvious buildings of the Rocky Mountain Health Ranch. This road has several steep switchbacks, so 4-wheel drive is recommended if there is much snow cover.

Elk Wallow Campground and Cunningham Creek Road

ELEVATION: 8,827 feet (Elk Wallow Campground)
10TH MTN MAP: Mount Yeckel
USGS MAP: Nast

Drive the above description for the Mountain Haven Trailhead. Instead of turning off and parking, simply continue up the left fork (North Fork Road) of the main road 2.6 miles to Elk Wallow Campground. To reach the Cunningham Creek Road, drive past Elk Wallow Campground for another 1.3 miles to a Y fork. The well-signed Cunningham Creek Road takes the right (S) tine of the fork.

Eagle & Vail Area Off I-70

Sylvan Lake Trailhead

ELEVATION: 8,558 feet
10TH MTN MAP: Burnt Mt.
USGS MAP: Crooked Creek Pass

Sylvan Lake is a popular ice fishing and snowmobile area. The road to the lake is well maintained, but may be temporarily closed during heavy storms.

Drive I-70 29 miles W from Vail or 30 miles E from Glenwood Springs and turn off at Eagle (Exit 147). Drive over the Eagle River, take a right on old Highway 6, and drive a short distance to Eagle. Turn left (S) on Broadway (the main street) in Eagle to 6th Street, turn left (E) on 6th, and drive one block to the Sylvan Lake (Brush Creek) Road. There are usually good signs marking this route through Eagle.

Turn right (S) on the Sylvan Lake Road and follow it for 10.6 miles to a well-signed fork (pavement ends here). Take the right fork (West Brush Creek Road) and drive 4.6 miles to Sylvan Lake. In the winter do not block the plow turn when parking.

Sylvan Lake is within a small state park. In the summer there is good car camping with bathroom facilities, and the park charges a small fee. There is good water at a spring .4 miles up the West Brush Creek Road.

Yeoman Park Trailhead

ELEVATION: 9,060 feet
10TH MTN MAP: New York Mountain
USGS MAP: Fulford

Follow the above directions for the Sylvan Lake Trailhead to get to the well-signed fork where the pavement ends on the Sylvan Lake Road. Take the left fork (East Brush Creek Road) and drive 5.8 miles to Yeoman Park. Turn right (SW) off the main road, and follow a spur a short distance down and over a bridge crossing East Brush Creek, then a few hundred feet to parking at snow closure in the campground.

West Lake Creek Trailhead

ELEVATION: 8,220 feet
10TH MTN MAP: New York Mountain
USGS MAP: Grouse Mountain

Because of poor signs, the drive to the West Lake Creek Trailhead is more intricate than most. Drive I-70 13 miles W from Vail or about 46 miles E from Glenwood Springs, and turn off at the Edwards Exit (Exit 163). Drive S for a short distance across the Eagle River to a stop sign and T intersection with highway 6. Turn right (W) and drive .7 miles to the poorly signed Lake Creek Road on the left (there may be a sign on a bus shelter here).

Drive the Lake Creek Road 1.9 miles to a well-signed Y intersection. Take a right (W) on the West Lake Creek Road and follow it 2.8 miles to a parking area where a switchback makes a hard left. The Card Creek drainage trail follows a distinct snow-covered road S from the parking area. 4-wheel drive may be necessary for the last part of West Lake Creek Road.

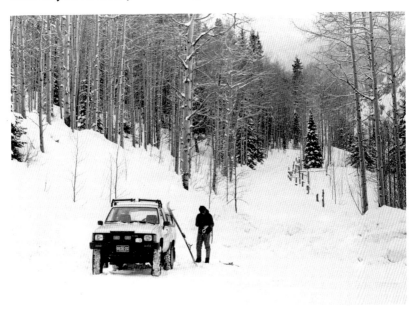

At the West Lake Creek Trailhead. The 10th Mountain suggested route follows the snow-covered road left of the fence.

Vail Trailhead for the Commando Run

ELEVATION: 8,220 feet
USGS MAP: Vail East

The Vail Trailhead for the Commando Run is not signed, but it's fairly easy to find. Follow I-70 to the main Vail Exit (Exit 176) at Vail Resort. Take the exit, then turn immediately right (S) into a 4-way stop intersection. Turn left (E) here on the frontage road and drive .4 miles E to an intersection marked with an oversized stop sign. Turn right (S) here and follow Vail Valley Drive .4 miles to parking at the Golden Peak Children's Skiing Center at the base of lifts 6 and 12. In the winter parking is highly regulated, so check the parking rules when you get there.

At any rate, you can skin up the ski area from here to start the Commando Run in Mill Creek. This is a grueling start for such a nice tour, so consider accessing the Commando Run from the Vail ski lifts. There has been talk for years of a one-ride ticket for just that purpose, so always check for this option. To reach the Commando Run from the lifts, you can get into Mill Creek from the top of lift 6; or you can take a more roundabout route, finally using the Orient Express Lift to reach the west ridge of Siberia Peak. In the summer, you can ride the Vail Gondola most of the way up the mountain, then hike the ridge to Siberia Peak. For cyclists, take your bicycle up the Gondola and you can ride from the top of the Gondola across the ski area to the Mill Creek Road.

Vail Pass Trailhead

ELEVATION: 10,610 feet
10TH MTN MAP: Resolution Mountain
USGS MAP: Vail Pass

As the second highest point on I-70, Vail Pass is known for its severe winter driving conditions. Take chain and snow tire laws seriously.

To reach the Vail Pass Trailhead, drive I-70 14 miles E from Vail or 5 miles W from Copper Mountain Resort. Take Exit 195 at the summit of the pass and park at the large parking area (the Vail Pass Rest Area) just east of the overpass. The Shrine Pass Road leaves from the parking area. It has good signage and is well used. Look out for snowmobiles.

Highway 24

Red Cliff Trailhead • Shrine Pass Road

ELEVATION: 8,680 feet
10TH MTN MAP: Resolution Mountain
USGS MAP: Red Cliff

Drive I-70 5 miles W from Vail Resort, or 55 miles E from Glenwood Springs, and take the Minturn Exit (Exit 171) onto U.S. Highway 24. Drive 11 miles S on Highway 24 to a poorly signed left turn-off that leads a short distance down into a canyon, then into Red Cliff. The Shrine Pass Road leaves from the NE corner of Red Cliff. It is poorly signed, but fairly obvious. You can ask any local where it is, and the USGS map shows it clearly as the only road up Turkey Creek. Pilgrim's Inn, which caters to cross country skiers, is located right at the trailhead.

Once you find the road, you have several parking choices. The best place to park, both for snowplowing and safety from theft, is in Red Cliff on any side street. The curb across from Reno's Bar is a good bet, and so is the Mexican food at Reno's. If you are on a day trip, drive just over a mile up the Shrine Pass Road to the snowplow turnaround at a water tank. You can park here for the day (put a note on your car), but don't park overnight.

Pando Trailhead • Elevation 9,200 feet
Camp Hale Trailhead • Elevation 9,250 feet
South Camp Hale Trailhead • Elevation 9,280 feet

10TH MTN MAP: Chicago Ridge
USGS MAP: Pando

These trailheads are located at the site of former Camp Hale – a huge, 3-mile long flat area on the Eagle River a few miles north of Tennessee Pass. Fifty years ago Camp Hale was home for two years to the men of the 10th Mountain Division of the U.S. Army,

for which the 10th Mountain trail system is named (see Appendix 2). Only road cuts and a few foundations remain.

Drive I-70 5 miles W from Vail Resort or 55 miles E from Glenwood Springs and turn off at the Minturn Exit (Exit 171) onto Highway 24. At 16 miles from the exit you will broach the huge flat area of Camp Hale. Look for a railroad siding to your right (the Pando siding), and a distinct parking area to your left with a sign reading Resolution Road. This is the Pando Trailhead.

To reach the Camp Hale Trailhead, continue from the Pando Trailhead 1.6 miles south on Highway 24. Look to your left for two stone gate posts and a plaque. This is the Camp Hale Trailhead; parking is obvious. There is no bridge across the Eagle River from the Camp Hale Trailhead; there may be a snow bridge, but don't count on it. For reliability, you may want to forgo using this trailhead and use the Pando Trailhead.

For the South Camp Hale Trailhead, continue S on Highway 24 for .7 miles past the Camp Hale Trailhead. Look to your left for another distinct parking area. Again, there is no bridge here, but due to the distance this trailhead can save you, it might be worth it to look for a snow bridge.

If you are coming from Leadville and Tennessee Pass, the South Camp Hale Trailhead is 5 miles north of Tennessee Pass on Highway 24. Use the connection mileages above to find the other two trailheads.

Tennessee Pass Trailhead

ELEVATION: 10,424 feet
10TH MTN MAPS: Chicago Ridge, Galena Mountain
USGS MAP: Leadville North

To reach Tennessee Pass from the north (I-70), follow the above directions for Pando Trailhead and Camp Hale. From Camp Hale continue S on highway Highway 24 for 7.3 miles to the well-signed Tennessee Pass. Parking is obvious on the west side of the road (opposite the turn-off to Ski Cooper).

From the south ("old town" in Leadville), follow Harrison Avenue (Highway 24) N, then follow signs for Highway 24. You'll pass through the strip development on the north end of town and come to an obvious left turn (W) for Highway 24 to Tennessee Pass. It's about 1 mile from "old town" to this turn. From the turn, follow Highway 24 8.8 miles to Tennessee Pass.

Crane Park Trailhead

ELEVATION: 10,137 feet
10TH MTN MAPS: Chicago Ridge, Galena Mountain
USGS MAP: Leadville North

From the north (I-70), follow the directions above to the Tennessee Pass Trailhead. Stay on Highway 24, and 1.6 miles past Tennessee Pass turn right (W) off the highway onto a dirt road. There is a sign here mounted on an antique road-grader for Webster's Sand and Gravel. Park at the snow closure. If the gravel pit is operating, the road will be plowed to there. You can then park at the well-signed intersection of the Wurts Ditch Road .9 miles from Highway 24.

From the south (Leadville) follow the directions under Tennessee Pass Trailhead to the turnoff toward Tennessee Pass. From the turn, follow Highway 24 (the following mileages are measured from this turn). At 2.3 miles you broach impressive Tennessee Park, with good views to the west of Galena Mountain and Homestake Peak. At 7.2 miles take a left onto the aforementioned road with the sign for Webster's Sand and Gravel to get to the trailhead.

Turquoise Lake Trailhead

ELEVATION: 9,880 feet
10TH MTN MAP: Galena Mountain
USGS MAP: Leadville North

Turquoise Lake is a beautiful reservoir several miles west of Leadville. It is a popular snowmobile recreation area. Thus, you'll have to share the parking and portions of trail with snow machines. Most importantly, if you park in a turnaround area, do so in a way that allows people with trailers to use it.

The trailheads around Turquoise Lake are simply snow closures on a continuous loop road. They vary with the season and the severity of storms, so you might find the road open several miles farther than the closures described below.

To reach the Turquoise Lake Trailhead, start from Leadville's Harrison Avenue in the historic "old town". Turn W onto West 6th Street and drive .8 miles to a T intersection with an obvious sign pointing right to the Turquoise Lake Recreation Area. Turn right and drive Lake County 4 to another well-signed right turn at 1.8 miles. The sign here points right and says Turquoise Lake North Portal (you are now on Lake County 9). Drive N then W over railroad tracks, then uphill to another T intersection at 3.9 miles. If this is snow closure, it is your trailhead. If not, turn right and continue to snow closure, which is often at 5.3 miles where the spur for the Tabor Boat Ramp turns left off the main road.

Chapter 2 • McNamara Hut

Built in 1983, the McNamara Hut was the second hut in the 10th Mountain system. The hut is a memorial to Margy McNamara (as Margy's Hut is as well). Funds to build the hut were donated by Margy's husband

ELEVATION:	10,360 feet
COUNTY:	Pitkin
TEXT MAP:	pp. 42-43
10TH MTN MAP:	Bald Knob
USGS MAP:	Thimble Rock
TRAILHEADS:	Hunter Crk., Lenado, Lenado Alternate

Robert, who served as secretary of defense. Located in Burnt Hole deep in the forest on the north side of Bald Knob (11,092 feet), the hut has a cozy secluded feeling that lends itself to sipping tea by the wood burner, or exploring the nearby forest on skis. There is good intermediate level ski touring on Bald Knob, and experts can strike out on long tours to the east towards the Continental Divide.

Back during the silver boom in the late 1800's, lumber for fuel, mine timbers, and building was a valuable commodity. As a result, the entire area around Burnt Hole, from Red Mountain to Bald Knob and east to Hunter Flats, was stripped of trees. Many sawmills operated in the area, including a Burnt Hole sawmill, the remains of which can still be seen east of the hut. During this period of logging, there were also fires that burned many acres; one such fire created Burnt Hole.

According to one old-timer, Widow Gulch (the watered drainage above the trail just west of Lenado Gulch) is named after widow Jennie Adair who operated a sawmill in the gulch. By all reports, she was quite a charac-

ter. For food, she would cut down a quarter of beef just large enough to fit in the cook stove oven (probably similar to the one in the McNamara Hut). After some roasting of the beef, she would trim away the done parts for a meal, put the roast back in the oven to supply the next day's meal, and so on. Her two bull dogs

10th Mountain Hut & Trail System

10th Mountain Trail is located in the White River
and San Isabel National Forests
under agreement with the Forest Service, USDA.

Scale 1:24,000

SCALE IN MILES

Vagneur
Mountain

Hut ■
Trailhead ●

Trails are marked by blue diamonds, except in
wilderness areas where trails are marked by tree blazes.

This map is not a substitute for good route-finding skills;
it is just an aid to help locate routes.
These are suggested routes only.
Trails are not groomed and their exact location may vary.

© 1989 • 10th Mountain Trail Association

WHITE RIVER NATIO

Larkspur
Mtn

3.03 m
3.25 m

3.2

RUEDI   MEREDITH
ASPEN   THIMBLE ROCK

Woody

Lenado   **Lenado Trailhead**
8540   8,640'

Campground

2.3

2.1
2.3

McNamara Hut
10,360'

1.88 miles to **McNamara Hut**
3.83 miles to **Hunter Creek Trailhead**

2.5

Red   Mountain

2.44 miles to **Hunter Creek Trailhead**
3.27 miles to **McNamara Hut**

2.1

Hunter Creek

1.00 miles to **Hunter Creek Trailhead**
4.71 miles to **McNamara Hut**

Hunter Creek Trailhead
8,380'

Parking

Aspen

Radio
Tower

42

continued on pp. 64-65 To Norrie

FOREST

Mtn

Mount
Yeckel

1.41 miles to **Margy's Hut**
6.16 miles to **Norrie**
6.78 miles to **McNamara Hut**

3.6

3.3
3.4

Foster Gulch

BM

Chapman

Margy's Hut
11,300'

BM
9805
2989

BM 2

3.7

11906
3628

2.4
3.1
3.5

Spruce Creek

Peak 12234

12268
3739

PROPOSED
SPRUCE CREEK ADDITION

3.51 miles to **McNamara Hut**
4.68 miles to **Margy's Hut**

2.62 miles to **McNamara Hut**
5.57 miles to **Margy's Hut**

2.6

11
3627

WILLIAMS MOUNTAINS

3897
2

HUNTER · FRYINGPAN WILDERNESS

Thimble
Rock

11844
3610

would clean up what was left. In those days, women wore dresses even while doing manual labor. While firing the sawmill boiler, Jennie's skirt would sometimes catch fire; she would just dunk it in a nearby water tub and keep working.

Compared to many other huts, the McNamara Hut has limited choices for ski routes. For ski-throughs, use route 2.4 north to Margy's Hut, or route 2.1 west to the Hunter Creek Trailhead. For branch routes, an ascent of Bald Knob is a nice jaunt, but one that can lack interest for experts. Hardcore bushwhackers can try route 2.6 — it is quite a challenge. For a quick ascent to the hut, route 2.1 is the most popular, mostly because it is near Aspen. Route 2.2 is slightly shorter, but leaves from a remote trailhead.

2.1

Hunter Creek Trailhead — McNamara Hut via Van Horn Park

DIFFICULTY: Intermediate
TIME: 6 hours up, 4 hours down
DISTANCE: 6 miles
ELEVATION GAIN: 2,000 feet; elevation loss: 20 feet
10TH MTN MAP: Bald Knob
USGS MAPS: Aspen, Thimble Rock

This 10th Mountain suggested route is the only practical way to get to the McNamara Hut from Aspen. Going the opposite direction, as a route from the hut to Aspen, it is usually the route of choice, though experts can ski to Aspen via Midway Pass (see *Colorado High Routes*). The Van Horn Park route follows old, well-defined logging roads, and is well marked with signs and blue diamonds. There are, however, several confusing junctions, and finding the trailhead can be trying. Use your maps. If you are starting from the Hunter Creek Trailhead, you'll soon need climbing skins, so put them on before you start.

ROUTE DESCRIPTION: For travel from Aspen to the hut, leave from the Hunter Creek Trailhead. Ski a fairly level trail NE through scrub oak 1/8 mile, then across the Benedict Bridge over Hunter Creek. From here, the trail climbs steeply for 3/4 mile on the south side of Hunter Creek, then breaks out into an open area at 8,600 feet elevation. Continue NE through low-angled open areas for 1/4 mile, then turn N and cross the 10th Mountain Bridge over Hunter Creek (8,640 feet). This bridge is well marked and easy to spot, but could be elusive in poor visibility. In that case, stay close to the stream past 8,600 feet elevation, and you'll bump into the bridge.

After crossing the 10th Mountain Bridge, continue N for a few hundred feet, then make a climbing traverse W (downvalley) to within sight of a sturdy fence and private home. Staying about 100 feet E from the fence, begin climbing N again, and you will intersect a clearly visible snow-covered jeep trail at about 8,720 feet. Now the real climbing begins. Follow the jeep trail as it takes you on a 1 1/3-mile climbing traverse to Lower Van Horn Park at Lenado Gulch. Take care not to turn left into Lenado Gulch. Just continue on an easterly tack across Lower Van Horn Park, through a gate (usually open), then climb NE through another aspen forest into Van Horn Park— a classic alpine "open space".

Read your map with care, and ski up the north side of Van Horn Park to Lower Van Horn Saddle (really just a low-angled shelf) at 9,760 feet. Continue along the north side of the park to Upper Van Horn Park, then Upper Van Horn Saddle, a more definitive saddle at 9,925 feet, just E of point 10,097.

From Upper Van Horn Saddle, ski easterly up a well-marked, narrow road cut through the forest. This road gradually climbs 2 miles to the Mc-Namara Hut. Generally, this trail is easy to follow. If you happen to catch it unbroken, use your compass and altimeter, and take care not to drop N down into the dense timber and steep terrain of the Woody Creek drainage. You'll usually smell wood smoke before you see the hut, as it is hidden by trees until you are within a few hundred feet.

REVERSE ROUTE DESCRIPTION: Reversing the route above is fairly simple. The crux is to get on the trail as you leave the cabin, as myriad ski tracks can be confusing. To be certain, take a compass bearing before you leave. It also helps to ask directions from new arrivals; but remember, they may be more bewildered than you are. After you're on the trail, you'll find a fast downhill traverse to Upper Van Horn Saddle. From there ski the fall line through Upper Van Horn Park. At the lower end of the park be sure to swing slightly left, and drop through trees into Lower Van Horn Park.

Just entering Van Horn Park on the way to McNamara Hut

Ski W across Lower Van Horn Park, re-enter the trees at the west end of the park, and find a distinct road cut that takes you on a "flying downhill" traverse into Hunter Creek. Cross the 10th Mountain Bridge over Hunter Creek, then continue downhill, gliding on a distinct trail that loosely follows the south side of the creek to the Benedict Bridge. Cross the Benedict Bridge and follow a short, low-angled trail through scrub oak to the Hunter Creek Trailhead and Hunter Creek Road. Enjoy Aspen.

SAFETY NOTES: This route has almost no avalanche danger, and is defiantly at the easier end of the intermediate rating. The steepest slopes in Upper Van Horn Park could avalanche, given extremely unstable snow. The downhills force you into some pretty narrow slots, so ski in control.

SUMMER: This route is an excellent hike, horse, or bike ride.

2.2

Lenado Trailhead — McNamara Hut via Woody Creek

DIFFICULTY: Intermediate
TIME: 5 ½ hours up, 5 hours down
DISTANCE: 5 ¼ miles
ELEVATION GAIN: 1,720 feet
10TH MTN MAP: Bald Knob
USGS MAPS: Aspen, Thimble Rock

As a route between trailhead and hut, this alternate trail is less popular than route 2.1, mostly because many people like the convenience of a trailhead closer to Aspen, but also because the lower 1 ½ miles of trail is not marked by 10th Mountain, and not open enough for easy skiing. Yet for just those reasons, you'll find more wilderness solitude on this route, and better map reading practice. Most skiers should use climbing skins for the ascent.

ROUTE DESCRIPTION: From the Lenado Trailhead, ski about ¼ mile up the road from the trailhead to a point just before an automobile bridge crossing Woody Creek (8,680 feet). On the right (E) side of the road you'll see some Forest Service trailhead signs. Leave the road here, and ski past the signs and up the Woody Creek drainage. Basically, the best route follows that of the pack trail marked on the USGS Thimble Rock map. Snow cover and low branches, however, may dictate some custom route finding. Your exact route up the drainage is not important, while drainage identification is. Using map, compass, and altimeter as you travel, spot Cliff Creek's confluence with Woody Creek. Continue up Woody Creek, and at the next confluence, that of Spruce Creek and Woody Creek, find the marked 10th Mountain trail on the north side of Woody Creek (9,440 feet). Note that a 10th Mountain suggested route leading to Margy's Hut (route 3.1) follows the Spruce Creek drainage from here.

Due to the well-maintained and marked 10th Mountain suggested route from here to the McNamara Hut, orienteering is easier above this point. One note, however: you won't see blue diamonds — this section of trail is marked with tree blazes. From the Spruce Creek confluence, follow the 10th Mountain marked trail another mile along the north side of Woody Creek. Stay on the trail as it crosses to the south side of Woody Creek (9,900 feet), then makes a switchback to the W, climbing up the south side of the Woody Creek drainage. This is perhaps the most critical juncture of the route, but it can be easily identified by careful altimeter use. Follow the switchback ½ mile W into a shallow gulch, then turn S and continue on the marked trail as it climbs the gulch to 10,240 feet. Here the trail turns and begins a westerly, gradually climbing traverse 2 miles to the McNamara Hut. The hut is visible from several hundred yards away.

REVERSE ROUTE DESCRIPTION: Leaving from the front porch of the Mc-Namara Hut, ski directly SW a few hundred feet, then swing E and follow a gradually dropping contour for 2 miles to 10,240 feet at a shallow gulch. Turn N and ski down the gulch (this can be difficult, use caution) to 9,960 feet. Stay on the trail as it turns and follows a dropping traverse E into the Woody Creek drainage, crosses Woody Creek, then follows the north side of the creek to Woody Creek's intersection with Spruce Creek. Here, the marked 10th Mountain suggested route continues up Spruce Creek to Margy's Hut (route 3.1).

To continue to the Lenado Trailhead, stay in the Woody Creek drainage. Ski the north side of Woody Creek for another mile or so, then cross the stream and ski the south side the next ½ mile to the automobile bridge mentioned above, then a short distance down the main road to the plow turnaround. Again, remember that the 10th Mountain suggested portion of this route is mostly marked with tree blazes, while the portion in lower Woody Creek has few markers of any sort.

SAFETY NOTES: With extremely unstable snow, there can be danger from bank sluffs on the steep sides of the Woody Creek drainage. These areas are easy to avoid, but pay attention. Be careful as you ski down into Woody Creek, as many tempting runs have stumps and rocks just under the surface of the snow.

SUMMER: This route is a fine hike, but horses should avoid the section from Woody Creek to the hut, as this trail is mostly just a marked winter route with no real path. Cyclists should note the wilderness boundary a short distance up Woody Creek from the trailhead.

2.3

Lenado Alternate Trailhead — McNamara Hut via Lenado Gulch

DIFFICULTY: Advanced
TIME: 7 hours up, 6 hours down
DISTANCE: 6 ½ miles
ELEVATION GAIN: 2,300 feet; elevation loss: 480 feet
10TH MTN MAP: Bald Knob
USGS MAPS: Aspen, Thimble Rock

This route follows classic, old-fashioned logging roads. Usually these are the perfect angle for hiking, horses, cycling, or mellow skiing — this one is no exception. Due to it's lack of "official" status, this is another lightly traveled trail that allows more solitude and requires more map work.

ROUTE DESCRIPTION: As is the case with many routes from trailhead to hut, the crux of this trip is finding the start of the trail. Use the description in Chapter 1 for "Lenado Alternate Trailhead".

On the trail, the going is mostly straightforward, but there are a few tricky spots. Put your skins on at the start. From the road, follow the trail for several hundred feet S, stay on the trail as it makes a left, then climbs E, then S, and switchbacks W. The trail then makes a long 2-mile climbing traverse W along the side of the Woody Creek valley, winding in and out of numerous small gulches to a turn left (S) around a shoulder at 9,700 feet. From here, turn S and follow the trail ⅓ mile as it passes first though open forest, then through a few open areas to a meadow at 9,800 feet. This is called Four Corners, and has a good sign (which may be covered by snow). Continue S downhill on a distinct road cut for 1 mile to a grove of aspens at the lower (W) end of Lower Van Horn Park (9,360 feet). Here you intersect route 2.1, which you follow to the McNamara Hut.

REVERSE ROUTE DESCRIPTION: From the McNamara Hut, take route 2.1 (reverse route) to the aspen grove at the west end of Lower Van Horn Park. Leave the marked route here, and turn right (N) onto the Lenado Gulch road cut. Climb 1 mile and 440 vertical feet to Four Corners. Start down the hill N from Four Corners, and identify the trail as it swings E to the side of the Woody Creek drainage. Stay on the trail as it takes a wild downhill traverse E into the Woody Creek valley, eventually dropping onto the Woody Creek Road a short distance from the winter plow turn.

SAFETY NOTES: See route 2.1. Take care at Four Corners to use your orienteering skills, many groups have become a bit bewildered here.

SUMMER: This route is terrific for all nonmotorized use.

2.4

McNamara Hut to Margy's Hut via Spruce Creek

DIFFICULTY: Intermediate   **ELEVATION GAIN:** 1,860 feet; loss: 920 feet
TIME: 8 hours   **10TH MTN MAP:** Bald Knob
DISTANCE: 8 ¼ miles   **USGS MAPS:** Thimble Rock, Meredith

This is the 10th Mountain suggested route from the McNamara Hut to Margy's Hut. For most of the tour, you'll be in dense conifer forest.

ROUTE DESCRIPTION: From McNamara Hut, follow route 2.2 (reverse route) to the Spruce Creek/Woody Creek confluence, where the Spruce Creek Trail intersects the Woody Creek Trail (9,400 feet). Keep a careful eye out for this junction, it's marked by 10th Mountain, but that's no reason to shirk your map duties. At the junction, put on your skins and ski N then NE up the well-defined, marked Spruce Creek Trail. You have a long pull ahead of you, as the trail follows follows the Spruce Creek drainage 3 ¼ miles and 1,560 vertical feet to the west end of Sawmill Park (11,000 feet).

As soon as you enter Sawmill Park keep a sharp eye out for another trail fork on your left. Many groups miss this junction–the trick is to identify Sawmill Park with adroit map reading, then stay at the lower (W) end of the park and carefully search out the 10th Mountain junction markers on a couple of medium-sized evergreens. An altimeter can really help here. If you've skied more than 50 feet into the open park, you have gone too far. Once you find the junction, leave the main trail and follow a spur W then SW as it makes a long 1 ¾-mile climbing traverse up to the hut. The hut is usually visible from a few hundred yards away; but it may be hidden by snow on heavy snow years, with just the upper front windows visible.

SAFETY NOTES: Be careful on the downhill into Woody Creek. Use care identifying the junction in Sawmill Park.

SUMMER: This route is a good hike, but most equestrians will find too much brush and deadfall for fun horse travel. Cyclists should note that this route is within designated wilderness, and thus is illegal for bicycles.

View from Bald Knob to the south

2.5

Bald Knob from McNamara Hut

DIFFICULTY: Intermediate
TIME: Several hours round trip
DISTANCE: 2 miles round trip

ELEVATION GAIN: 732 feet round trip
10TH MTN MAP: Bald Knob
USGS MAP: Thimble Rock

This is the most popular branch route for skiers staying at the McNamara Hut. The spectacular view of the Elk Mountains from Bald Knob (11,092 feet) makes up for McNamara Hut's lack thereof, and the skiing is great.

ROUTE DESCRIPTION: From the hut's front porch ski to the water hole, then continue SW up the left side of the stream shown on the USGS map. At about ¼ mile swing left and climb S up open areas with burnt trees, then through a grove of evergreens to Bald Knob's summit. Enjoy the view of the Elk Mountains and try to spot Margy's Hut which is visible from several spots near the Bald Knob summit. For downhill skiing check out the aforementioned open areas, or explore glades to the E of the summit, taking care to traverse back to the hut before dropping into Slab Park.

SAFETY NOTES:

Remember that Bald Knob is not a maintained ski resort! There are plenty of hidden obstacles and sudden drop-offs. Ski in control.

SUMMER:

This is a beautiful wildflower hike. There is no real trail for mountain bikes or horses. The wilderness area boundary runs N/S through the summit.

2.6

Williams Mountains from McNamara Hut

DIFFICULTY: Expert
TIME: Very long day
DISTANCE: 14 miles round trip

ELEVATION GAIN: 2,890 feet round trip
10TH MTN MAP: Bald Knob
USGS MAP: Thimble Rock

There are few options for peak climbs from McNamara Hut. The alpine ridge nearest the hut is miles away, with an approach through heavy timber that can make the best orienteer weep. Skilled ski mountaineers still enjoy trying this route, and several have made it. All groups attempting this route should have a map, compass, altimeter, and avalanche transceivers.

ROUTE DESCRIPTION: To begin, take route 2.5 to the summit of Bald Knob. Get out your map on the summit and do some careful planning, with the following description as a guideline. Ski E than NE down Bald Knob into the upper end of Slab Park (10,600 feet). Put skins on here, then climb E into Horse Park, then ski to the far east end of Horse Park. Use compass and map here to climb E on to a bumpy, timber-studded ridge that climbs 2 miles to the summit of point 11,900 (a good goal in itself), then drops another ¾ miles E to a saddle at 11,500 feet. Be very careful with your orienteering on this ridge, as you'll be in some dense timber. It may be possible to save some work by contouring the south side of point 11,900.

Climb E from the saddle and you'll soon break timber line and be on a beautiful west face dropping from the Williams Mountains ridge. Before you climb to the ridge, spend some time doing your avalanche evaluation. This slope is often wind-scoured and safe, but it can be loaded with unstable snow. Depending on conditions, hike or ski the 650 vertical feet from timber line to the ridge top. The return is via the same route, perhaps with a traverse below Bald Knob to save energy.

SAFETY NOTES: This route requires expertise in all aspects of winter mountaineering, hence its expert rating. You'll find little problem with avalanche danger until the final open slope on the Williams Mountains ridge, where you should use extreme caution. Turn back if you have doubts.

SUMMER: This route begins in heavy timber that makes for difficult hiking. The Williams Mountains ridge, however, is a worthy summer objective. To avoid some of the timber you can use the pack trail shown dropping from the 11,500-foot saddle. Even still, the route is long and strenuous.

Chapter 3 • Margy's Hut

Built in 1982, Margy's Hut (along with the McNamara Hut) was one of the first two in the 10th Mountain system. It represented a major milestone for the fledgling organization, which had to

ELEVATION: 11,300 feet
COUNTY: Pitkin
TEXT MAP: pp. 42-43, 64-65
10TH MTN MAP: Bald Knob, Mt. Yeckel
USGS MAP: Meredith
TRAILHEADS: Lenado, Norrie

promise the Forest Service that the huts would be razed if they were not used.

Located on a lightly treed hillside just below timber line, Margy's Hut has beautiful views of the Elk Mountains to the south. The area around the hut was heavily logged in the mid 1900s, but there is still a rare stand of virgin timber east of the hut. Margy's was built with funds given by Robert McNamara (former secretary of defense) and friends, in memorial to Margy McNamara, Robert's wife.

There is good downhill skiing close to the hut, and several fine branch routes lead into the surrounding mountains. Mount Yeckel (route 3.6) is the most popular place for downhill skiing, and there is a good run from the front porch of the hut. For ski-throughs to the north, most skiers use the Twin Meadows route (3.3/3.4) which drops into the Fryingpan River drainage. You can ski to accommodations in the Fryingpan at the Rocky Mountain Health Ranch and the Diamond J Guest Ranch. Ski-throughs south from Margy's usually follow Spruce Creek (route 3.5). The shortest route from a trailhead to Margy's Hut climbs from Lenado via Johnson Creek (route 3.2).

3.1
Lenado Trailhead — Margy's Hut via Spruce Creek

DIFFICULTY: Intermediate
TIME: 6 hours up, 4 hours down
DISTANCE: 6 1/2 miles
ELEVATION GAIN: 2,660 feet
10TH MTN MAP: Bald Knob
USGS MAPS: Aspen, Thimble Rock, Meredith

As a route between trailhead and hut, this alternate trail is less popular than route 3.2, mostly because the lower 1 1/2 miles of trail is not marked by 10th Mountain and not well cleared for skiing. Yet, for just those reasons, you'll find more wilderness solitude on this route, and you'll get better map reading practice. Use climbing skins for the ascent.

ROUTE DESCRIPTION: From the Lenado Trailhead, ski about ⅓ mile up the road to a point just before an automobile bridge crossing Woody Creek (8,680 feet). On the right (E) side of the road you'll see some Forest Service trailhead signs. Leave the road here and ski past the signs and up the Woody Creek drainage. Basically, the best route follows that of the pack trail marked on the USGS Thimble Rock map. Snow cover and low branches, however, may dictate some custom route finding. Your exact route up the drainage is not important, while drainage identification is. Using map, compass, and altimeter as you travel, spot Cliff Creek's confluence with Woody Creek. Continue up Woody Creek, and at the next confluence, that of Spruce Creek and Woody Creek (9,440 feet), find the marked 10th Mountain trail junction on the north side of Woody Creek.

Keep a careful eye out for this junction; it is marked by 10th Mountain, but that's no reason to shirk your map duties. From the junction ski N then NE up the well-defined and marked Spruce Creek Trail. You have a long pull ahead of you, as the trail follows the Spruce Creek drainage 3 ¼ miles and 1,560 vertical feet to the west end of Sawmill Park (11,000 feet).

When you enter Sawmill Park keep a sharp eye out for another trail fork to the left. Many parties miss this fork. If you have trouble, the trick is to identify Sawmill Park with adroit map reading. Stay at the lower (W) end of the park and carefully search out the 10th Mountain junction markers on a couple of medium-sized evergreens. An altimeter can really help here as well. If you ski more than 50 feet into Sawmill Park, you are past the junction. Once you find the junction, follow the spur W then SW as it makes a long 1 ¾-mile climbing traverse up to the hut. The hut is usually visible several hundred yards before you reach it, but it may be hidden by snow on heavy snow years, with just the upper front windows showing.

REVERSE ROUTE DESCRIPTION: Follow route 3.5 (reverse route) from Margy's Hut down Spruce Creek to Woody Creek. Descend on the north side of Woody Creek. At the Cliff Creek confluence cross to the south side of Woody Creek and continue down Woody Creek to the road and auto bridge mentioned above. Take a left (S) at the road and ski the road to the Lenado Trailhead.

SAFETY NOTES: Bank sluffs are possible on the steep sides of the Woody Creek drainage; however, these slopes are easy to skirt. This route includes two major junctions on what has been called the "Hidden Marker Trail" by some frustrated skiers. Remember that, due to it's location within designated wilderness, the trail is marked with tree blazes.

SUMMER: This route is fine for horseback riding or hiking. Most of the route is within designated wilderness, so cyclists should use other trails such as the Larkspur Mountain Road (see Chapter 1, Lenado Trailhead).

3.2

Lenado Trailhead — Margy's Hut via Johnson Creek Trail

DIFFICULTY: Intermediate
TIME: 5 ½ hours up, 4 hours down
DISTANCE: 6 miles
ELEVATION GAIN: 2,660 feet
10TH MTN MAP: Bald Knob
USGS MAPS: Aspen, Meredith

This 10th Mountain suggested route is the "Interstate Highway" route to Margy's Hut. It is well marked, and follows distinct road cuts and trails.

ROUTE DESCRIPTION: From the Lenado Trailhead at the road's snow closure, ski up the main road ⅓ mile across an automobile bridge over Woody Creek. Stay on the wide road cut of the main road for 1 mile to a distinct left switchback (9,068 feet). Put your skins on here. Just before the switchback, turn right off the main road and climb a steep hill. You will be following a more ill-defined road cut on the east side of Silver Creek. At 9,270 feet turn right (E) out of the Silver Creek drainage and follow a sidehill trail that climbs (with several switchbacks) 1 ½ miles up Johnson Creek to another distinct snow-covered road at 10,480 feet.

Turn right (S) on this obvious road which leads slightly downhill and level for ¼ mile (leave your skins on) around a shoulder, and then gradually climbs for 2 miles to 11,040 feet. Here, the 10th Mountain suggested route takes a left fork (switchback) and climbs N 180 vertical feet to a timbered saddle. From the saddle ski several hundred feet N and intersect another snow-covered road on the north side of the saddle.

Turn right (E) on this road and follow it for ½ mile as it traverses north-facing terrain. Just before the road makes a turn N, leave the road and ski SE through a clearing, then a short distance downhill to the hut. The hut is not visible until you are several hundred feet away.

Many skiers like to take a more direct route from the 11,040-foot elevation. To do so, simply stay on the jeep trail as marked on the USGS Meredith map, then deviate slightly to contour the south side of the bump W of the hut, then traverse to the hut. Take care not to drop below the hut (use your altimeter).

REVERSE ROUTE DESCRIPTION: From the back of Margy's Hut, ski NW up a short hill, then continue a few hundred feet to intersect a distinct snow-covered road. Follow this road SW for ½ mile, then turn left to leave the road and climb over a low saddle. Ski 180 vertical feet down the south side of the saddle. Try to stay on the 10th Mountain marked route, but if your downhill speed forces you to deviate, just be sure to get back on the trail as it turns S then W, then gradually drops (with a few level sections and a short uphill) 2 miles to the head of Johnson Creek. Ski the trail down Johnson Creek into Silver Creek, then to the Lenado Trailhead.

SAFETY NOTES: This is a well-marked trail. Nevertheless, you will be traversing some steep, heavily timbered mountainsides, where losing the route could be grim. Pay attention. While most of the trail is free of avalanche danger, there is one obvious steep gulch you cross while in the Johnson Creek drainage. Avalanches are rare here, but parties should still use standard precautions.

SUMMER: These trails provide good cycling, hiking, and horse riding. Cycling up the Johnson Creek route is quite strenuous, but it is a terrific advanced downhill. Cyclists should consider using the Larkspur Mountain Road for the trip up.

3.3

Norrie Trailhead — Margy's Hut via Twin Meadows

DIFFICULTY: Intermediate
TIME: 8 hours up, 6 ½ hours down
DISTANCE: 7 ½ miles
ELEVATION GAIN: 2,917 feet; elevation loss: 57 feet
10TH MTN MAP: Bald Knob
USGS MAP: Meredith

While adventurous skiers might find other routes from the Fryingpan drainage to Margy's Hut, this 10th Mountain suggested route is certainly the most popular line. You can also begin this route at the Diamond J Guest Ranch Trailhead (see route 4.1).

ROUTE DESCRIPTION: From snow closure at the Norrie Trailhead, ski up the well-defined cut of the Twin Meadows Road. It makes two switchbacks, then a 1¾-mile climbing traverse to 9,300 feet. Leave the road here and turn right (SE) onto a fairly narrow, marked trail that leads to the north end of Twin Meadows at 9,465 feet. Many skiers use wax up to this point, then put on their skins.

Follow a marked trail cut along the west side of Twin Meadows. Stay on the trail as it leads out of Twin Meadows on the north side of Deeds Creek, then crosses Deeds Creek and climbs into Foster Gulch. The trail next parallels Foster Creek for ½ mile, then begins to turn W away from Foster Creek at 9,920 feet, and climbs W to 10,240 feet. From here you swing S then W to meadows at 10,400 feet.

From the meadows a steep climb leads over a divide (11,057 feet) and into Sawmill Park. Enjoy the view of the Elk Mountains from Sawmill Park and ski down to the lower (W) end of the park. At the lower end of the park (11,000 feet) keep a sharp eye out for another trail fork to the right. It is easy to miss this fork, as many people can attest. If you have trouble, the trick is to identify Sawmill Park with adroit map reading, then stay on the north side of the park and ski to the west end where you search out the 10th Mountain junction markers on a couple of medium-sized evergreens. Your altimeter can really help here.

Once you find the junction, leave the main trail and follow a spur W then SW as it makes a long 1¾-mile climbing traverse up to the hut. The hut is usually visible several hundred yards before you reach it, but it may be hidden by snow on heavy snow years, with just the upper front windows visible.

REVERSE ROUTE DESCRIPTION: Skiing this route from Margy's to the trailhead is simple. The traverse from Margy's Hut drops you into Sawmill Park, where you can find the marked trail by simply skiing to the saddle at the upper (E) end of the park. You then ski a well-marked trail down Foster Gulch and along Deeds Creek to Twin Meadows. Ski NE then N along the west side of Twin Meadows, then N through trees until you hit the distinct snow-covered road that traverses N to the Norrie Trailhead.

SAFETY NOTES: Most trail markers on this route are tree blazes. There is no avalanche danger. The long walk through the forest can lull you into a trance, so take extra care in Sawmill Park to find the correct route.

SUMMER: Hikers and equestrians will enjoy this route. Cyclists are not permitted due to designated wilderness.

3.4

Rocky Mountain Health Ranch Trailhead — Margy's Hut

DIFFICULTY: Intermediate
TIME: 9 hours up, 7 hours down
DISTANCE: 8 ¾ miles
ELEVATION GAIN: 2,740 feet; elevation loss: 200 feet
10TH MTN MAP: Mount Yeckel
USGS MAPS: Nast, Meredith

This 10th Mountain suggested route uses most of the same trail as 3.3 from the Norrie Trailhead. It has slightly less elevation gain, but more miles.

ROUTE DESCRIPTION: Begin at the Rocky Mountain Health Ranch Trailhead, with skins. From the main lodge at the ranch, ski or walk (depending on snow cover) 500 feet SW on the ranch road to the last two cabins at the end of the road. The trail starts here in aspen trees between the two cabins. The trail cut is not obvious.

Ski the trail SW another 500 feet to a foot bridge over a small creek (8,800 feet). Cross the creek, then swing W and climb ¼ mile up a steep gulch to a flat area (9,010 feet). The South Fork of the Fryingpan River will be directly in front of you at the bottom of a shallow gulch. Turn left (S then SW) and follow a trail cut that parallels the South Fork for just under ¼ mile to cross the South Fork (no bridge) at 9,050 feet.

After crossing the South Fork, the trail winds W then SW for several hundred yards to a vague Y split. Here, one trail continues up the South Fork of the Fryingpan, while the one you want climbs to the right (W) up a small hill, then winds 1/3 mile (light uphill) through conifer and aspen to a major road (9,150 feet). If you lose the trail here, just continue W and you'll intersect the road. Once you're on the road (road number 504.1), you simply follow snow-covered roads W for 3 1/4 miles to intersect route 3.3 at Twin Meadows.

In detail, from the trail/road intersection, ski NW and W as the road climbs gradually for 1 mile, then drops slightly and swings around a shoulder to a T intersection with road 504.1A and 504. Turn right (W) on road 504 and follow it as it climbs gradually for 3/4 mile around another shoulder, then drops gradually 1/4 mile to another intersection at 9,500 feet. Be sure you take the left (W) road at this intersection; it leads 1/8 mile and about 100 vertical feet down into the north end of Twin Meadows. Ski W across the north end of Twin Meadows and find 10th Mountain suggested route 3.3 that follows the west side of the meadows. Take a left (S) and follow route 3.3 to Margy's Hut.

REVERSE ROUTE DESCRIPTION: Start without skins at Margy's Hut. Follow route 3.3 (reverse route) to Twin Meadows. At the north end of the meadows, ski to the east side of the meadows, then up a road cut that climbs 1/8 mile through timber to intersect the major road cut of road 504. Ski road 504 1 mile to another major intersection. Take a left (N) on road 504.1, and ski the road gradually uphill around a shoulder, then down a long gradual downhill 1 mile to 9,160 feet.

Here, the trick is to find a not-so-obvious pack trail that drops into a forest of small aspen trees from the east side of the road. There might be 10th Mountain trail markers here, but use these to verify your careful orienteering, rather than blindly searching for markers.

This trail leads downhill SE then E to cross the South Fork of the Fryingpan River at 9,050 feet. You then parallel the river on your left for 1/4 mile to a small flat opening (9,020 feet). Here, you must swing right (E) and ski into a small subsidiary gulch. This gulch steepens and leads you to a foot bridge over a small creek (8,800 feet). Cross the bridge (can be obscured by snow) and ski N 500 feet through aspen forest to the Rocky Mountain Health Ranch. Enjoy your dinner!

SAFETY NOTES: There are no overt dangers on this route, but skiers should note the length of the trail and plan accordingly.

SUMMER: This whole route is a fine hike or horse ride. The section of trail from road 504.1 down to the Rocky Mountain Health Ranch is a rough bicycle downhill, and mostly a portage in the opposite direction. The network of dirt roads make fabulous bicycle routes. Cyclists should note the wilderness boundaries.

3.5

Margy's Hut to McNamara Hut via Spruce Creek

DIFFICULTY: Intermediate
TIME: 6 hours
DISTANCE: 8 miles
ELEVATION GAIN: 920 feet; elevation loss: 1,860 feet
10TH MTN MAP: Bald Knob
USGS MAPS: Meredith, Thimble Rock

For good downhill skiers, this 10th Mountain suggested route is one of the quicker hut to hut routes. Novice downhillers, however, should plan on some slow moving down Spruce Creek.

ROUTE DESCRIPTION: From the east side of Margy's Hut, climb NE up a short hill, and follow the marked (tree blazes) 10th Mountain suggested route as it makes a long traverse into Sawmill Park. Expert parties have reported skiing directly SE from the hut down into the Spruce Creek drainage, but they encountered difficult timber towards the bottom. Anyone but the most expert skier should stick to the trail.

When you enter Sawmill Park, turn immediately right (W) and begin your descent SW down Spruce Creek on a 10th Mountain suggested route with standard tree-blaze markings. This section of trail is relatively straightforward. Ski 3 miles down Spruce Creek to the intersection with the Woody Creek Trail (9,440 feet). Take care to identify this junction. Turn left (E) onto the Woody Creek Trail (still marked by blazes) and follow the north side of Woody Creek 1 mile to 9,900 feet. Cross Woody Creek.

Due to the well-maintained and marked 10th Mountain suggested route from here to the McNamara Hut, orienteering is easier above this point, but skiers addicted to blue diamonds will still have to squint as they look for tree blazes. After crossing Woody Creek, stay on the trail as it makes a switchback to the W, climbing up the south side of the Woody Creek drainage. Follow the switchback ½ mile W into a shallow gulch, then turn S and continue on the trail as it climbs the gulch to 10,240 feet. Here the trail turns and begins a westerly, gradually climbing traverse 2 miles to the McNamara Hut. The hut is visible from several hundred yards away.

SAFETY NOTES: Watch for possible bank-sluff danger on the steep sides of the Woody Creek drainage. Ski in control while descending Spruce Creek.

SUMMER: Because of wilderness designation, cyclists are not allowed on this route. Hikers will find all the trails described above to be good, but they should note that the section between the McNamara Hut and Woody Creek is not really a path, it is just a marked route for winter skiing. Horse riders should note the same.

3.6

Mount Yeckel from Margy's Hut

DIFFICULTY: Intermediate to Advanced
TIME: ½ day round trip
DISTANCE: 2 ¼ miles round trip
ELEVATION GAIN: 465 feet round trip
10TH MTN MAP: Mount Yeckel
USGS MAP: Meredith

Good views, plenty of downhill skiing, close to a hut: could you ask for more? This is the most popular branch route from Margy's Hut, and it includes something for everyone. Be sure not to miss this route.

Touring to Mount Yeckel

ROUTE DESCRIPTION: From the back of Margy's Hut, ski the 10th Mountain marked trail about 200 yards to a distinct snow-covered road. Instead of following the 10th Mountain route left, turn right and travel the general route of the road N through an open area, then E over point 11,648. From here, follow a snow-covered jeep trail NE down a short hill, then up to the summit of Mount Yeckel. The return is via the same route.

You'll find excellent downhill skiing in the north-facing bowl of point 11,648; this is known as Yeckel Bowl. There is also good skiing off the summit of Mount Yeckel down the open west face; this is called the West Face of Yeckel.

SAFETY NOTES: There is ski touring on this route for any ability level. All downhillers should ski with care; avalanches are common in Yeckel Bowl. The West Face is slightly less avalanche prone. Stay away from Yeckel's steep, cliff-studded northeast face.

SUMMER: This is a good hike and horseback ride. Expert cyclists will enjoy it as well, but they should note the wilderness boundary just a few feet south of the jeep trail. The summit of Yeckel is also within wilderness, so be sure to leave your bike behind for the last hundred feet to the summit. Possession of a bicycle in designated wilderness is a crime punishable by confiscation of the bicycle and a fine.

3.7

Peak 12,234 from Margy's Hut

DIFFICULTY: Advanced
TIME: 5 hours round trip
DISTANCE: 7 miles round trip
ELEVATION GAIN: 1,534 feet round trip
10TH MTN MAP: Mount Yeckel
USGS MAP: Meredith

While enjoying the view from the Margy's Hut picture window (or outhouse), many a mountaineer has pondered Peak 12,234. Every year several groups make the ascent, and by all reports it is a worthwhile objective. While not the accessible ski area that Mount Yeckel is, Peak 12,234 has good views, a bit of turning on the way back down, and plenty of navigation practice.

ROUTE DESCRIPTION: To begin, ski from Margy's Hut to Sawmill Park (see route 3.3). Put your skins on here. From the park, use map and compass to ski SE to point 11,250. This area is densely timbered, so don't expect any definitive landmarks. From point 11,250 climb SE up a broad timbered ridge; your goal is the large meadows northwest of peak 11,904. Again, pay attention to your map, compass, and altimeter. Ski to 11,400 feet at the bottom of the meadows. Next, climb the southwest edge of the meadows to the 11,650-foot saddle W of point 11,904. Climb the ridge to the summit of Peak 12,234. Return is via the same route.

SAFETY NOTES: Though there is little or no avalanche danger on the route described above, there is plenty of slide terrain on the sides of Peak 12,234. Thus, groups planning on "adult" skiing should carry avalanche transceivers and know their avalanche safety techniques. This is a branch route with no trail markers.

SUMMER:
Due to heavy timber with no trail cut or tread, this route would be a poor choice in the summer.

Chapter 4 • **Fryingpan Drainage**

The Fryingpan River drainage is a major east/west drainage that separates the Aspen area from the Eagle area to the north. Many routes connect the Fryingpan drainage with 10th Mountain huts. In the past, the traditional stopover in the drainage was the Diamond J Guest Ranch. Now, the Rocky Mountain Health Ranch is providing lodging as well. In addition, there is lodging in the

ELEVATION: 8,250' (Diamond J), 8,760' (Health Ranch)
COUNTY: Pitkin
TEXT MAP: pp. 64-65, 72-73
10TH MTN MAP: Mt. Yeckel, Burnt Mt.
USGS MAP: Meredith (Diamond J), Nast (Health Ranch)
TRAILHEADS: Spring Creek, Diamond J Ranch, Mountain Haven, Elk Wallow Campground, Norrie, Rocky Mountain Health Ranch

gateway town of Basalt. Other private accommodations are planned for this area, so call 10th Mountain for the latest information.

The Diamond J Guest Ranch is the oldest and most charismatic of the Fryingpan's choices in lodging. In the Colorado Midland Railroad days of the late 1800s, the ranch location was known as Muckawanago, after a Ute Indian word meaning "Where the bear walks". A nearby creek is still called Muckawanago Creek. There was a ticket office on one side of the creek, and a railroad station. Built as a shorter line in competition with the Denver and Rio Grande, this section of the Midland stretched from Basalt, up the Fryingpan drainage, and over Hagerman Pass to the Leadville area. The line was famed for the "big trestle", an incredible span built completely with wooden timber. Just to house the service people, a whole town existed under the trestle.

The Colorado Midland Railroad closed down in 1918, and Muckawanago was bought in 1927 by Delbert and Thelma Bowles. They registered the Diamond J brand (uses a reverse J) and operated several guest cabins. Presently, the ranch is owned by a group of stockholders. The Muckawanago station building is now the hay barn. In the tradition of the great Colorado guest ranches, the Diamond J Guest Ranch offers full-service lodging with all-season road access. For 10th Mountain hut skiers the lodge rents several rustic cabins. Amenities include showers, sauna, and Jacuzzi. Meals are available as well.

The Rocky Mountain Health Ranch (originally called the Horseshoe Bend Ranch) is located at 8,760 feet in the Fryingpan drainage, 5.4 miles up the main paved road from the Diamond J Guest Ranch. The Rocky Mountain

Health Ranch consists of a main lodge and a number of outbuildings. Skiers stay in the main lodge. Meals, showers, and bedding are provided. There is little alpine mountaineering near the ranch and few places for downhill skiing. There are, however, myriad touring trails nearby that use a network of summer trails and snow-covered dirt roads. These roads were built for a monstrous water diversion project, and now serve as terrific recreation access.

Since the Fryingpan drainage lodging is not in the backcountry, but on a road, most of the routes described in this chapter leave from trailheads near the lodging. The Spring Creek, Mountain Haven, and Elk Wallow Campground trailheads can be reached from the Diamond J Guest Ranch and Rocky Mountain Health Ranch by taking the Fryingpan Road (see Chapter 1). You have myriad choices for routes out of "The Fryingpan". If you're headed north to the Harry Gates Hut use route 4.4, it is shorter than route 4.5, and is used by fewer snowmobiles. The most expedient route south to Margy's Hut is route 4.1 from the Norrie Trailhead. For branch routes, use routes 4.6 and 4.7 or the first part of route 4.3 to explore the country at the head of the drainage. The latter route is the longest in this guide, and is seldom skied.

4.1

Fryingpan Drainage (Diamond J Guest Ranch) to Margy's Hut via Twin Meadows

DIFFICULTY: Intermediate
TIME: 8 3/4 hours
DISTANCE: 9 1/4 miles
ELEVATION GAIN: 3,107 feet; elevation loss: 57 feet
10TH MTN MAP: Mount Yeckel
USGS MAP: Meredith

While adventurous skiers might find other routes from the Fryingpan drainage to Margy's Hut, this 10th Mountain suggested route is certainly the most popular line.

10th Mountain Hut & Trail System

10th Mountain Trail is located in the White River
and San Isabel National Forests
under agreement with the Forest Service, USDA.

Scale 1:24,000

SCALE IN MILES

Hut
Trailhead

Trails are marked by blue diamonds, except in
wilderness areas where trails are marked by tree blazes
This map is not a substitute for good route-finding skills.
You must be able to help locate routes.
These are suggested routes only.
Trails are not groomed and their exact location may vary.
© 1989 10th Mountain Trail Association

Avalanche Peak

HOLY CROSS WILDERNESS

Slim Jim Gulch

Telluride Park

5.8

5.9

To Peter Estin Hut   continued on pp. 72-73

1.80 miles to Harry Gates Hut
3.70 miles to Crooked Creek Pass
5.13 miles to Peter Estin Hut
via Little Lime Creek Ridge Trail

To Peter Estin Hut

To Crooked Creek Pass

3.30 miles to Crooked Creek Pass
5.60 miles to Spring Creek

BM 2944
2847

Lime Park

Coral

JEEP TRAIL

Harry Gates Hut
9,700'

Choker Cutoff

Burnt Mtn

5.7

2.20 miles to Harry Gates Hut
4.40 miles to Mountain Haven

CROOKED CREEK PASS

MOUNT JACKSON

MEREDITH
MAST

BM 9609

2.30 miles to Mountain Haven
3.70 miles to Harry Gates Hut

4.4
5.1

Burnt Mountain Road

4.4
5.1

0.40 miles to Harry Gates Hut

Lime Canyon

1.40 miles to Spring Creek

3.60 miles to Spring Creek

BM 6767 2979

4.5
5.2

Eagle Road

Spring Creek Trailhead
CR 400
BM 8395
2559

Nelson

Montgomery Flats

INDEFINITY

PACK TRAIL

Middle Gulch

Suicide Gulch

Thomasville

BM 7989

Bessie Park

Frying Park TRAIL

64

WHITE RIVER
NATIONAL FOREST

Cunningham Creek

Diemer Lake

Sellar Lake

Sellar Park

BM
10330
3067

BM

BM 9145
2787

Norrie Trailhead
8,440'

1.45 miles to Diamond J Ranch

Norrie

Gravel
Pit

Road 504

Twin
Meadows

Rocky Mountain
Health Ranch
Trailhead
8,760'

Last

2.92 miles to Norrie
4.25 miles to Rocky Mountain Health Ranch
4.65 miles to Margy's Hut

BM 991.4
3022

BM
9994
3055

Chapman

BM

PACK

SAWYER

Chamberlin Gulch

Foster Gulch

Teterum Ridge

HUNTER - FRYINGPAN WILDERNESS

Cyclone
Mtn. 7,788

Mine

Mount
Yeckel

Margy's Hut
11,300'

To McNamara Hut

1.41 miles to Margy's Hut
6.16 miles to Norrie
6.78 miles to McNamara Hut

continued on pp. 42-43

| 4.7 |
| 4.3 |
| 13.2 |
| 4.6 |
| 3.4 |
| 4.2 |
| 4.1 |
| 3.3 |
| 3.3 |
| 3.4 |
| 4.1 |
| 4.2 |
| 3.7 |
| 2.4 |
| 3.1 |
| 3.5 |
| 3.6 |
| 3.2 |

ROUTE DESCRIPTION: Follow the well-defined ski trail on the south side of the road from the Diamond J Guest Ranch 1 ¾ miles to the Norrie Trailhead. For the remainder of the trail, see route 3.3.

4.2

Fryingpan Drainage (Rocky Mountain Health Ranch) to Margy's Hut via Twin Meadows

DIFFICULTY: Intermediate
TIME: 9 hours
DISTANCE: 8 ¾ miles
ELEVATION GAIN: 2,740 feet; elevation loss: 200 feet
10TH MTN MAP: Mount Yeckel
USGS MAPS: Nast, Meredith

This route connects with the 10th Mountain suggested route 4.1 for the popular tour to Margy's Hut. It is fairly long, and has several devious sections of trail. Get an early start.

ROUTE DESCRIPTION: See route 3.4.

4.3

Fryingpan Drainage to Uncle Bud's Hut via Hagerman Pass

DIFFICULTY: Advanced
TIME: Very long day or overnight camp
DISTANCE: 21 miles (from Elk Wallow Campground Trailhead)
ELEVATION GAIN: 4,881 feet; elevation loss: 2,328 feet (from Elk Wallow Campground Trailhead)
10TH MTN MAPS: Mount Yeckel, Galena Mountain
USGS MAPS: Homestake Reservoir, Mt. Massive, Nast, Meredith

This alternate trail connects the Leadville 10th Mountain huts with the Fryingpan River drainage. It is the only route in this book that crosses a high pass, and thus will attract "alpine" wilderness skiers. Future plans call for several more huts near this route. At this time the trail is long and arduous.

ROUTE DESCRIPTION: Follow directions to the Elk Wallow Campground Trailhead (Chapter 1). For a description of the remainder of the way to Uncle Bud's Hut see route 13.2.

4.4

Fryingpan Drainage to Harry Gates Hut via Burnt Mountain Road

DIFFICULTY: Novice
TIME: 5 ½ hours (from Mountain Haven Trailhead)
DISTANCE: 6 ½ miles (from Mountain Haven Trailhead)
ELEVATION GAIN: 1,844 feet; elevation loss: 464 feet (from Mountain Haven Trailhead)
10TH MTN MAP: Burnt Mountain or Mount Yeckel
USGS MAP: Meredith, Crooked Creek Pass

This 10th Mountain suggested route is the shortest and easiest route to the Harry Gates Hut. It is mostly a walk through the forest and on a logging road that passes under a major power line several times (good for map reading). There are several good glimpses of the Elk Mountains to the S. Climbing skins are useful for the first 4 ½ miles of travel to the high point on the Burnt Mountain Road. You can strip skins here, wax the next 1 ¾ miles, then herringbone a short hill to the hut.

ROUTE DESCRIPTION: Follow the Fryingpan Road to the Mountain Haven Trailhead (see Chapter 1). For a description of the remainder of the trip to the hut see route 5.1.

4.5

Fryingpan Drainage to Harry Gates Hut via Lime Park

DIFFICULTY: Novice
TIME: 8 hours (from Spring Creek Trailhead)
DISTANCE: 8 miles (from Spring Creek Trailhead)
ELEVATION GAIN: 1,630 feet; elevation loss: 370 feet (from Spring Creek Trailhead)
10TH MTN MAP: Burnt Mountain or Mount Yeckel
USGS MAPS: Meredith, Crooked Creek Pass

This long route follows a well-used snowmobile trail on the Eagle Road which connects the Fryingpan drainage with Sylvan Lake and Eagle. With suitable snow you can use cross country wax. Some of the "fit and fleet" use skins or wax for the initial climb, then skate the flats through Lime Park.

ROUTE DESCRIPTION: Drive the Fryingpan Road to the Eagle Road (.9 miles NW of the Diamond J Ranch) and follow the directions in Chapter 1 to the Spring Creek Trailhead. See route 5.2 for the trail description.

4.6

Sellar Lake from Elk Wallow Campground

DIFFICULTY: Novice
TIME: 6 hours round trip
DISTANCE: 7 miles round trip
ELEVATION GAIN: 1,370 feet round trip
10TH MTN MAP: Mount Yeckel
USGS MAP: Nast

This short branch route is a fine jaunt. Go for a picnic, or practice your winter camping close to civilization.

ROUTE DESCRIPTION: From the Elk Wallow Campground Trailhead ski S ¼ mile across the bottom land to the point where obvious power lines start up the mountain side. Put your skins on here, and ski up the well-defined road cut that begins a few feet S of the power lines. After about a mile of snow-covered road, you will reach Diemer Lake.

From the north side of Diemer Lake follow an obvious road cut E as it switchbacks under the power lines a few times and leads to the top of a timbered shoulder at 10,050 feet. From here continue a gradual climb on the snow-covered road for another mile to Sellar Lake (10,210 feet). Return via the same route.

SAFETY NOTES: There is no avalanche danger on this route. Yet, do not let the novice rating lead you into a bad situation. Even a novice ski touring route requires some map reading, the correct timing, and proper equipment, not to mention a minimum overall skill level.

SUMMER: The roads in the vicinity of these lakes make good bicycle, horse, and hike routes. Also, try for some trout if you like.

4.7

Sellar Peaks Traverse from Elk Wallow Campground/ Cunningham Creek Road

DIFFICULTY: Expert
TIME: 9 hours round trip (from Cunningham Creek Road)
DISTANCE: 13 miles round trip (from Cunningham Creek Road)
ELEVATION GAIN: 3,015 feet round trip
10TH MTN MAP: Mount Yeckel
USGS MAP: Nast

This long branch route is perfect for a day in April or early May. It includes two summits, enjoyable and safe downhill skiing, and one of the best views in the Sawatch Mountains. It is a good choice if you are staying at any of the lodging in the Fryingpan drainage.

ROUTE DESCRIPTION: There are two ways to begin the Sellar Peaks Traverse; your choice depends on whether the North Fork Road (Chapter 1, Elk Wallow Campground Trailhead) is open only as far as Elk Wallow Campground, or another 1.25 miles to its intersection with the Cunningham Creek Road.

(Start number 1) From Elk Wallow Campground follow route 4.6 to Sellar Lake, then connect with the route described below. Though not as direct as start number 2, you can do this any time of year.

(Start number 2) This option saves you about 380 feet of elevation gain and about two miles, but depends on your being able to drive up from Elk Wallow Campground to the Cunningham Creek Road. This section of road opens up sometime in late April or early May, depending on the year's snowfall.

From the intersection of the North Fork Road and the Cunningham Creek Road (9,210 feet), follow the Cunningham Creek Road for 1 3/4 miles to 9,520 feet. Leave the road here, cross Cunningham Creek (can be a wade in the spring), then head up the hill about 680 vertical feet to Sellar Lake. Due to heavy timber, it can be hard to navigate directly to the lake. Don't worry about this, because as long as you're in the general area of the lake you can continue climbing to the next part of the route — the 10,441-foot saddle on the ridge that divides the Cunningham drainage from the Fryingpan drainage. From the saddle, stay on the ridge and climb through medium density timber to timber line, then to the summit of West Sellar Peak (12,074 feet).

At the summit enjoy the awesome views of Mt. Massive, Avalanche Ridge, the Red Tables, and the Elk Range. Then, if you're ambitious, make a short ski run to the SW for six hundred vertical feet. Regain the ridge between the two summits and use it as your route (1 mile) to the east summit.

For an excellent downhill run from the east summit, ski down the southeast shoulder for about 600 vertical feet (staying away from the cornice), then take a northerly contour to the 11,320-foot saddle that the power lines pass through.

From the saddle, ski the line cut and nearby glades all the way down to the dogleg turn in the lines (10,560 feet). Be careful of avalanches in a couple of the steeper parts of the line cut. You can bypass these by skiing the glades to the E.

After the dogleg, continue down the powerline to the low point just before the line crosses Middle Cunningham Creek. Take a right (N) turn out of the low point and travel an obvious road cut down to the Cunningham Creek Road. Travel back down the Cunningham Creek Road to the North Fork Road.

SAFETY NOTES: On heavy snow years, watch for low hanging power lines. There may be pocket slide danger in several gullies on the descent. You can avoid these with simple traverses.

SUMMER: The Sellar Peaks are a worthy destination, but the routes described above require too much bushwhacking for summer use.

Near the summit of Sellar Peak. Looking southeast at Mt. Massive, 14,421 ft.

Chapter 5 • Harry Gates Hut

Built in 1986, the Harry Gates Hut was the fourth cabin added to the 10th Mountain system. It is the largest of the 10th Mountain owned huts, with three floors that can sleep 20 people (reservations limited to 16). Indeed, many people

ELEVATION: 9,700 feet
COUNTY: Eagle
TEXT MAP: pp. 64-65, 72-73
10TH MTN MAP: Mt. Yeckel, Burnt Mt.
USGS MAP: Crooked Creek Pass
TRAILHEADS: Spring Creek, Mountain Haven, Sylvan Lake

feel it is too big, and more recent 10th Mountain huts have been scaled down. Inside, you'll find two kitchens: one main kitchen and one reserved for guided groups and hut maintenance people. Plenty of windows look out on the sunsets and the spectacular Avalanche Ridge. The hut was built with funds from the Gates Foundation in memorial to the late Harry F. Gates, who was an outdoorsman with a deep love for the mountains.

The hut is located in a clearing on a small wooded knoll, at the lowest elevation of any 10th Mountain hut. This makes the cabin easy to get to, but curtails access to the higher mountains east and northeast of the hut. Nonetheless, those skiers with the skill and endurance will find the Avalanche Ridge east of the hut to be a worthy objective (route 5.8). If you like to explore, the Tellurium Park area (route 5.9) is also an attractive branch trip. Skiers who want to stay closer to the hut, and novices, can use Burnt Mountain (route 5.7) as an accessible playground. The trip to the summit of Burnt Mountain is a terrific initiation into ski climbing.

With the exception of the Lime Ridge Trail to the Peter Estin Hut (route 5.5), the 10th Mountain suggested routes connecting the Harry Gates Hut to other huts and trailheads use snow-covered roads. Since these roads are heavily used by snowmobiles, they are usually packed, so bring some picnic food and your lightweight skis — you're bound to have a great time. So far, snowmobilers and skiers have co-recreated with few problems. This will continue if people practice a few common courtesies. Simply put, snow-mobilers should slow down while near skiers, and skiers should step to the side to let them by.

The quickest route to the Harry Gates Hut is via the Montgomery Flats connection to the Burnt Mountain Road (route 5.1). The long, scenic route is the ski from Sylvan Lake (route 5.3) — a tour recommended only for the hearty.

If you're pushing towards Aspen from the Harry Gates Hut, you have a choice of spending a night at the Diamond J Ranch, or continuing to Margy's Hut. The Diamond J is so close via a downhill of route 5.1, that you can easily spend the morning touring around the hut or exploring some route variations on the way down. If you're on a long trip, this is a opportunity for an "active rest day". If you plan on skiing through the Fryingpan drainage to Margy's Hut, you're looking at more than 16 miles of skiing with almost 4,000 feet of elevation gain.

If you're headed towards Vail, use the Lime Ridge Trail (route 5.5) for the fastest 10th Mountain suggested route to the Peter Estin Hut. For an even more direct route, advanced skiers can use the Lime Drainage Trail (route 5.6). For a scenic cruise use route 5.4, but start early.

5.1

Mountain Haven Trailhead — Harry Gates Hut via Burnt Mountain Road

DIFFICULTY: Novice
TIME: 6 hours up
DISTANCE: 7 miles (including walk from parking at Diamond J)
ELEVATION GAIN: 1,844 feet; elevation loss: 464 feet
10TH MTN MAP: Mount Yeckel or Burnt Mountain
USGS MAPS: Meredith, Crooked Creek Pass

This 10th Mountain suggested route is the shortest and easiest route to the Harry Gates Hut. It is mostly a walk on a logging road through the forest. The road passes under a major power line several times (good for map reading). There are several good glimpses of the Elk Mountains to the south. Climbing skins are useful for the first 4 1/2 miles of travel to the high

Aerial view of the Harry Gates Hut from the west.

point on the Burnt Mountain Road. You can strip skins here and wax the next 1 ¾ miles, then herringbone a short hill to the hut.

ROUTE DESCRIPTION: Begin the route with climbing skins at the Mountain Haven Trailhead. From the road closure gate at the trailhead, ski a logging road NW a short ways across a clearing, then into an aspen forest. Follow the road as it climbs NW about ½ mile to 8,400 feet, switchbacks around a small knoll, then climbs SE before turning N to 8,840 feet. This spot has been dubbed Overlook Point — it's a good place to strip some clothing and get a drink.

From Overlook Point, continue up the obvious road cut. After another 400 vertical feet of climbing along ½ mile of trail, you will broach a low-angled area known as Montgomery Flats. Stay on the road NE through Montgomery Flats for 1 ½ miles to a junction with the Burnt Mountain Road at 9,450 feet. The Burnt Mountain Road is a wide, distinct road cut. Use your altimeter and the power lines for precise navigation.

From the junction, the 10th Mountain suggested route follows the Burnt Mountain Road as it takes a northerly tack with several switchbacks for

1 ½ miles to the road summit at 10,030 feet. You can navigate by how many times you pass under the power lines — four times to the road summit. However, if you use skins it makes sense to cut the two main switchbacks on the way up. In fact, with good snow conditions and skilled orienteering, advanced skiers have found that a more direct ascent route and better skiing on the way down are possible by using the general route of the pack trail to the W of Silver Creek, as marked on the USGS Meredith map.

From the road summit (10,030 feet) the 10th Mountain suggested route continues along the Burnt Mountain Road for another 1 ¾ miles to a clearing at 9,566 feet. Consider removing your skins at the road summit and applying some cross country wax for this glide through the beautiful evergreen forest. At the clearing, turn right (NE) off the road and ski ¼ mile (134 vertical feet) NE up the hill from the road, unlock the door of the hut, and make tea.

One major variation of this route makes sense for advanced skiers traveling to the hut. From the road summit mentioned above, leave your skins on, stay on the road, and ski from the summit down a short hill and around the shoulder of point 10,224. Just as the Burnt Mountain Road begins to head N, leave the Burnt Mountain Road and ski up an obvious logging road that cuts through the trees NE. The Choker Cutoff, as this shortcut is called, traverses for a mile to skiable glades on the west side of Burnt Mountain. Strip your skins here. Good skiers can make turns most of the way from here to the Harry Gates Hut. Be careful not to get lost in the woods. Most likely, there will be tracks leading to the hut from the glades.

REVERSE ROUTE DESCRIPTION: For travel from the Harry Gates Hut to the trailhead, it's easy to reverse the above directions. The whole trip can be done using cross country wax. You can get some turns in by cutting the switchbacks on the Burnt Mountain Road. Farther down, hold a strong snowplow through the section below Overlook Point!

SAFETY NOTES: There is no avalanche danger on this route. Ski in control on the descent, as any wild falling will put you into a tree. Orienteering on the 10th Mountain suggested route is relatively easy. Variations should only be navigated by advanced skiers.

SUMMER: The Burnt Mountain Road makes an excellent, but strenuous, bike ride, run, or hike. Cyclists should avoid the Montgomery Flats section because of navigation difficulties and private land. Instead, they should use the Burnt Mountain roadhead. This is reached by continuing past Mountain Haven on the road to Elk Wallow Campground (see Chapter 1). At 2.2 miles past Mountain Haven (.4 miles before the campground) you will see the well-signed Burnt Mountain Road to the left (N).

5.2

Spring Creek Trailhead — Harry Gates Hut via Lime Park

DIFFICULTY: Novice
TIME: 8 hours up, 5 hours down
DISTANCE: 8 miles
ELEVATION GAIN: 1,630 feet; elevation loss: 370 feet
10TH MTN MAP: Mount Yeckel or Burnt Mountain
USGS MAPS: Meredith, Crooked Creek Pass

This long route follows a well-used snowmobile trail on the Eagle Road (see route 5.3) which connects the Fryingpan drainage with Sylvan Lake and Eagle. With suitable snow you can use cross country wax for the whole trip. Some of the "fit and fleet" use skins or wax for the initial climb, then skate the flats and enjoy the downhills through Lime Park.

ROUTE DESCRIPTION: Start at the Spring Creek Trailhead. Ski N up the obvious road cut 3 ½ miles and 1,090 vertical feet to the huge open area of Lime Park (9,560 feet). You can identify your entrance into Lime Park by passage under the power line shown on the USGS Crooked Creek map.

Skirt the west edge of Lime Park for another ½ mile past the power line (still on the road). If you're using skins remove them here, then swing E and follow the road down a wide ravine to 9,313 feet. Continue on the road as it turns N to its intersection with the Burnt Mountain Road. Take care to identify this intersection; there is a sign, but it may be covered by snow.

To continue to the Gates Hut (you're still in Lime Park) turn SE onto the Burnt Mountain Road. The road will lead you across a short flat area for about ¼ mile, then down a hill to the intersection with the Woods Lake Road at 9,270 feet. Again, whatever your direction of travel, use this intersection as a critical destination in your navigation. Stay on the Burnt Mountain Road as it takes you downhill another ⅛ mile and crosses Lime Creek at 9,190 feet.

At the crossing apply some cross country wax or skins if needed, and climb the Burnt Mountain Road a short distance E, then ½ mile S to a clearing at Slim Jim Gulch. Follow the road S another ¼ mile to a smaller clearing at 9,566 feet. At this point, turn left off the Burnt Mountain Road and ski NE 134 vertical feet up a hill to the hut. You cannot see the hut from the road, so pay attention!

REVERSE ROUTE DESCRIPTION: If you are heading from the hut to Lime Park, the Burnt Mountain Road is obvious at first, but can be hard to find in Lime Park. When you exit from the west side of Lime Park be sure to use the road, as a false trail could lead you into dangerous Lime Creek Canyon. The power line and an altimeter reading will set you on the correct track.

SAFETY NOTES: Keep your ears open for snowmobiles. (See notes for route 5.3)

SUMMER: The road from the Spring Creek Fish Hatchery is a fine mountain bike ride. This whole area is beautiful for hiking, biking, or horseback riding. The Eagle Road, from the Hatchery to Sylvan Lake (and beyond), is passable for 2-wheel drive autos with high clearance when it is dry. Even 4-wheel drive vehicles have been stuck on this road when it gets wet.

5.3

Sylvan Lake Trailhead — Harry Gates Hut via Crooked Creek Pass

DIFFICULTY: Intermediate
TIME: 11 hours up, 7 hours down
DISTANCE: 10 ½ miles
ELEVATION GAIN: 1,952 feet; elevation loss: 810 feet
10TH MTN MAP: Burnt Mountain
USGS MAP: Crooked Creek Pass

This gorgeous 10th Mountain suggested route is probably the least used trail to the Harry Gates Hut, simply because it is longer than other routes, and the trailhead is farther from population centers. Wait until late winter or early spring, click into your light touring rig, and spend a day on this route. You will be rewarded by a pleasant cruise through the forests, good views from Crooked Creek Pass, and some downhill turns in Lime Park. The trail is almost always packed by snowmobilers.

ROUTE DESCRIPTION: To begin, drive to the Sylvan Lake Trailhead. From your parking at snow closure, ski up the distinct snow-covered West Brush Creek road cut for a mile around the north and east sides of the lake, then on up into the Brush Creek valley for 4 ¾ miles to Crooked Creek Pass. Use your altimeter to identify the switchbacks at 9,220 feet and 9,260 feet, then the turn at 9,450 feet. From here be certain to stay on the road as it climbs S then SE around a timbered ridge dividing Spine Creek from Brush Creek, and then continues paralleling Brush Creek to Crooked Creek Pass (10,005 feet). Crooked Creek Pass is fairly distinguishable, but an altimeter check is always a good idea.

From Crooked Creek Pass ski the road 1 mile SE to Crooked Creek Park.

Ski into Crooked Creek Park (you may be able to get a few turns here), then follow the Crooked Creek drainage (stay on the road if in doubt) to the obvious dam, buildings, and flat expanse of Crooked Creek Reservoir. Ski the road on the dam along the west side of the reservoir, then about ¾ of a mile down the Little Lime Creek drainage (still on the road) to Lime Park and a well-signed, obvious road junction (9,280 feet). Pay attention to your compass and altimeter to navigate to this point.

Now you will be standing at the north edge of Lime Park, a vast clearing that can make for confusing navigation on the best of days. The way to handle Lime Park is to look for the road cuts and signs at road junctions, but continue to heed your compass and altimeter.

From the 9,280-foot junction, ski the road SE across Lime Park to its intersection with the Woods Lake Road, then downhill S to cross Lime Creek at 9,190 feet. Next, take care to identify and follow the Burnt Mountain Road as it climbs into the timber after crossing Lime Creek.

Ski up the Burnt Mountain Road ½ mile to a large clearing at the base of Slim Jim Gulch (9,440 feet). Ski the road S across the clearing, then nip through the trees (still on the road) for another ¼ mile to a smaller clearing at 9,566 feet. Turn left (NE) off the road here and climb several hundred yards NE up a knoll to the Harry Gates Hut. The hut is visible from about halfway up the knoll.

REVERSE ROUTE DESCRIPTION: The crux is navigating across Lime Park up to Crooked Creek Reservoir. The road cut from the reservoir up to Crooked Creek Pass is easy to find. Once you are on Crooked Creek Pass, the snow-covered road is obvious all the way to the Sylvan Lake Trailhead. If you lose the road, the drainage will still lead you to the lake.

SAFETY NOTES: There is little avalanche danger on this route. Some of the steeper slopes in Lime Park have avalanched during very unstable conditions. Bank sluffs have been observed along the road from Crooked Creek Reservoir to Lime Park. Take care with navigation through Lime Park, and by all means stay out of Lime Creek Canyon.

SUMMER: All the roads used by this route provide fabulous mountain bike riding, hiking, and running. Avoid holiday weekends or you will be coughing up dust for months. A good mountain bike ride takes the power line road from Crooked Creek Pass back S to its intersection with the Eagle Road (see route 5.2).

5.4

Harry Gates Hut to Peter Estin Hut via Crooked Creek Pass

DIFFICULTY: Expert
TIME: 10 ½ hours
DISTANCE: 10 miles
ELEVATION GAIN: 2,275 feet; elevation loss: 775 feet
10TH MTN MAP: Burnt Mountain
USGS MAPS: Crooked Creek Pass

Arduous miles, intricate route finding, rewarding vistas, and the sense of really covering the country—that sums up this fabulous hut to hut ski tour (10th Mountain suggested route).

ROUTE DESCRIPTION: Get an early start from the Harry Gates Hut and ski the 10th Mountain suggested route ¼ mile SW to the Burnt Mountain Road, or ski down the hill behind the hut N to the Slim Jim Gulch clearing and the Burnt Mountain Road. The latter route saves time for good downhill skiers.

Follow the Burnt Mountain Road downhill to the Lime Creek stream crossing at 9,190 feet elevation. You will now be in the midst of Lime Park, a huge open area that has confounded the best navigators. The best route through the park follows the road (portions may be obscured by snow) as it climbs and winds about ⅛ mile NW to the intersection with the Woods Lake Road. Do not take the Woods Lake Road. Stay on the Burnt Mountain Road another ½ mile W then NW to its intersection with the Eagle Road (9,300 feet). This is your critical intersection. Both intersections are marked by good signs, but they could be covered by snow. Your compass, map, and altimeter will insure positive identification.

Turn N on the Eagle Road as it leads up Little Lime Creek to the dam and obvious flat area of the Crooked Creek Reservoir. Stay on the road as it climbs past the reservoir up the north side of Crooked Creek Park, then enters the aspen trees at 9,650 feet, and continues 1 ½ miles to Crooked Creek Pass (10,005 feet).

Now the real climbing begins. Leave the Eagle Road at the summit of the pass by heading NW up an obvious road cut (starts on the W side of a fence) that climbs just over ¼ mile to a switchback, then SE to another switchback, then around the west shoulder of point 11,087. The road, still an obvious cut, then follows a long traverse on the north side of point 11,087, then drops 260 vertical feet to a saddle near the head of Spine Creek (10,700 feet).

Stay on the road from the saddle for another ⅛ mile NE to the switchback as shown on the USGS Crooked Creek Pass map (10,760 feet). Leave the road here and climb E ¼ mile and 90 vertical feet to the top of the ridge separating Spine Creek from Little Lime Creek. Here your route converges with the Lime Ridge Trail (route 5.5) and continues N up a well-marked route through a sparsely timbered logged area to Hat Creek Saddle (11,120 feet). This is the broad saddle just W of the Peter Estin Hut. You cannot see the Peter Estin Hut from Hat Creek Saddle, and you can ski past the hut if you are not paying attention. To guard against this, use your altimeter and map to identify Hat Creek Saddle. Swing E here, and when you break through a grove of pines the hut will be obvious.

SAFETY NOTES: There are many points along this route where a navigation mistake will send you down the wrong drainage. So be certain that at least one member of your party is a good orienteer. Some of the steeper slopes in Lime Park avalanche on rare occasions, and bank sluffs have been observed on the road cuts. Whiteout conditions are common in Lime Park.

SUMMER: The Eagle Road is easy mountain bike riding. The road from Crooked Creek Pass up into Spine Creek is strenuous but ridable. A good ride leaves from Crooked Creek Pass, then takes the Spine Creek road up to the three-trail confluence just west of the Peter Estin Hut, then down the Hat Creek logging roads (see route 6.2). The Ironedge Trail (route 6.3) is a perfect downhill ride for mountain bike experts. All the trails in this area are fine for running, hiking, and equestrian use.

5.5

Harry Gates Hut to Peter Estin Hut via Lime Ridge Trail

DIFFICULTY: Intermediate
TIME: 8 hours
DISTANCE: 7 miles
ELEVATION GAIN: 2,130 feet; elevation loss: 630 feet
10TH MTN MAP: Burnt Mountain
USGS MAP: Crooked Creek Pass

This is the most scenic and direct 10th Mountain suggested route between the Harry Gates Hut and Peter Estin Hut.

ROUTE DESCRIPTION: Leaving from the Harry Gates Hut, follow route 5.4 to the Woods Lake Road intersection (9,270 feet) in Lime Park. The road here may be obscured by snow, but the signs and fence break are usually obvious. Put your skins on here. Use your compass to follow the trail (marked on the USGS Crooked Creek Pass map) that climbs N up through a clearing, then through timber to the crest of the ridge separating Lime Park from Crooked Creek Reservoir. Follow the trail NE along the ridge (the trail cut is not obvious) for ¾ mile. Turn N and travel through timber, then down into the Little Lime Creek drainage. This circuitous route avoids private land around Crooked Creek Reservoir.

Cross the east fork of Little Lime Creek at 9,680 feet, take a perpendicular course from the creek, and contour 1/2 mile NW up the west fork of Little Lime Creek. At about 9,700 feet cross the creek and switchback S up to the crest of the ridge (Lime Ridge) separating Middle Creek from the west fork of Little Lime Creek. Once on the crest of Lime Ridge, follow a well-marked and fairly distinct trail cut that leads through intermittent clearings and timber to 10,150 feet.

Continue up the ridge as the timber thickens, and follow a well-defined trail cut through Sherwood Forest to a low-angled area with mature aspen trees. Take a look at the interesting old initials carved in these trees. Continue N, switchback, then climb steeply through clearings and dark timber to another low-angled area at 10,850 feet. From here continue N ¾ mile through a sparsely timbered logged area to Hat Creek Saddle (11,120 feet), a nondescript divide between the Hat Creek drainage and the west fork of Little Lime Creek. Travel E from the saddle several hundred yards to the hut. It is not visible directly from the saddle, but soon becomes obvious.

SAFETY NOTES: This trail is usually safe from snowslides, though steep slopes on the ridge sides could be dangerous during extremely unstable periods. Of more concern should be route finding and the length of the trip.

SUMMER: This trail is not recommended for cycling. Equestrians and hikers will find much to explore in this area, but the actual Lime Ridge Trail was cut several years ago only for winter use. Thus, there is no real path to follow (see route 5.6).

5.6

Harry Gates Hut to Peter Estin Hut via Lime Drainage Trail

DIFFICULTY: Advanced
TIME: 7 hours
DISTANCE: 6 ¼ miles
ELEVATION GAIN: 2,130 feet; elevation loss: 630 feet
10TH MTN MAP: Burnt Mountain
USGS MAP: Crooked Creek Pass

Though best as a descent from Peter Estin Hut to Harry Gates Hut (route 6.6), this route also serves as a direct climbing route for the glycogen depletion crowd (it cuts ¾ mile of the 10th Mountain suggested route 5.5). If that puts fire in your quads, bear in mind the fact that this not being a 10th Mountain suggested and marked trail, it is less likely to be broken. If you have to, it's easy to abandon this trail and use route 5.5.

ROUTE DESCRIPTION: To begin, Follow route 5.5 to the west fork of Little Lime Creek (9,700 feet). To follow the Lime Drainage Trail, simply say on the route of the pack trail that follows the gut of the drainage, rather than switchbacking up onto Lime Ridge (see route 5.5). Stay in the drainage (veer to either side of the creek for easiest travel lines) for about 1 ½ miles and 900 vertical feet to the bottom of steep open slopes at 10,600 feet. Head left (W) into the trees if you suspect avalanche danger and follow the edge of the timber or route 5.5 the remainder of the way to the Peter Estin Hut. If there is little avalanche danger you can stay on the open slopes and follow the crest of an obvious rib up to a point directly below the hut.

SAFETY NOTES: Heed the possibility of avalanche danger on the slopes just below the Peter Estin Hut, and on steeper sections of other open glades lower in the drainage.

SUMMER: Hikers and equestrians can use the pack trail as marked on the USGS Crooked Creek Pass map. Cyclists will find this trail too steep and inconsistent for good riding.

5.7

Burnt Mountain from Harry Gates Hut

DIFFICULTY: Intermediate
TIME: 3 hours round trip
DISTANCE: 4 miles round trip
ELEVATION GAIN: 1,558 feet round trip
10TH MTN MAP: Mount Yeckel or Burnt Mountain
USGS MAPS: Crooked Creek Pass, Mount Jackson

Some say that the only thing better than skiing this branch route to the summit of Burnt Mountain would be a night in a hut on top—what a location! With a full panorama of views, perfect ski glades, and beautiful gnarled stumps and trees, this place is a "must see". Catch a sunrise or sunset if you can (bring a head lamp for the latter).

ROUTE DESCRIPTION: Start with skins. From the Harry Gates Hut, ski directly SE a few hundred feet and down into a ravine. Ski into the forest on the southeast side of the ravine, then ski almost due S to the toe of a long Y-shaped clearing that leads up the west side of Burnt Mountain. Optionally, you can stay in the forest to the NE of the clearing until you hit the pack trail (called the Choker Cutoff) that contours at 10,200 feet. Choker Cutoff is easily identified by its cut through the trees and a well-defined trail shelf that shows through the snow cover (can be obscured during heavy snow years).

From Choker Cutoff the route is simple; climb the Y clearing to its top at 10,600 feet, continue up for a few hundred yards through light timber to the summit clearing, then continue up through the summit clearing to the summit at 11,178 feet.

You can get some good skiing by heading back down the ascent route, or try some tree skiing to either side of the clearings. Trap crust is common on these exposures. If you encounter this dread condition try the slopes on the N and NE side of the summit. If you are more into covering ground than making turns, try a high orbit of the summit at about 10,800 feet or do the Tellurium Park Loop (route 5.9).

SAFETY NOTES: Take care to ski in control while skiing the trees. There can be avalanche danger on the steeper slopes dropping from the summit, and cornices can form on occasion.

SUMMER: Burnt Mountain is an excellent summer hike. You'll encounter some light bushwhacking if you leave directly from the Harry Gates Hut. For an easier route, take Choker Cutoff from the Burnt Mountain Road, then ascend the pack trail as marked on the USGS Crooked Creek Pass map. The first few miles of Choker Cutoff from the Burnt Mountain Road are actually a logging trail and can be ridden on a mountain bike. The summit pack trail is too steep and inconsistent for bicycle use.

5.8

Avalanche Peak from the Harry Gates Hut

DIFFICULTY: Expert
TIME: 12 hours round trip
DISTANCE: 13 miles round trip
ELEVATION GAIN: 3,741 feet round trip
10TH MTN MAP: Mount Yeckel
USGS MAPS: Crooked Creek Pass, Mount Jackson

While many mountain skiers feel the pull of ascent fever as they ponder Avalanche Peak (12,803 feet) from the comfort of the Harry Gates Hut, few go to the summit. Only experts should attempt this long, involved tour. Even hardened mountaineers should only attempt the peak during very low avalanche hazard, preferably in the late winter or spring when the snowpack has consolidated. The route requires detailed orienteering through the Tellurium Park area. You'll get in plenty of downhill skiing as well as a real summit on this route.

ROUTE DESCRIPTION: There are two options to start the route, both end up at Tellurium Lake. If you want the best views and skiing, follow route 5.7 to the summit of Burnt Mountain, ski the glades on the northeast face of Burnt Mountain down to Tellurium Park, then swing through the park to Tellurium Lake. Navigation in this area is tricky, but taking time with compass, map, and altimeter will get you there. Using the other start, climb Burnt Mountain to Choker Cutoff at 10,200 feet (see route 5.7), then ski Choker Cutoff to the pack trail leading up into Tellurium Park and on to Tellurium Lake. The intersection of Choker Cutoff and the pack trail (10,240 feet) is not obvious, so pay close attention to your orienteering.

The real fun begins at Tellurium Lake. From the north end of the lake head N for about ¼ mile, then climb E to a small clearing starting at 10,660 feet. Climb to the top of this clearing, then continue climbing up a poorly defined shoulder and through several more clearings to timber line at about 11,500 feet. You may find discouraging bushwhacking up to this point, but stick with it. The idea is to get to timber line so you can travel through sparser trees and see where you're going. Once at timber line be careful of avalanche exposure as you contour N along the trim line for ½ to ¾ mile to the west shoulder that drops from the peak's summit. There is no obvious ridge line, so take care to identify the best route to follow the shoulder to the summit. In times of low avalanche danger (probably best in spring) you can wander up the west face.

For your descent, ski the west face if avalanche conditions allow, or follow ridges and ribs for an avalanche avoidance route down to timber line. Retrace your route to Tellurium Park, then take Choker Cutoff or Slim Jim Gulch (see route 5.9) back to the Harry Gates Hut. It is tempting to descend Slim Jim Gulch from the peak, but only the most expert skiers will be able to handle the dense bushwhacking that this entails.

SAFETY NOTES: Start early, bring a head lamp, and remember your emergency bivouac gear. Be very careful of avalanche danger on the above-timberline portion of this route. There is no true ridge line that totally avoids potential avalanche slopes.

SUMMER: This is a fairly good hike, though there is no real trail between Tellurium Lake and the summit.

5.9

Tellurium Park Loop from Harry Gates Hut

DIFFICULTY: Intermediate
TIME: Full day round trip
DISTANCE: 7 miles round trip
ELEVATION GAIN: 1,800 feet round trip
10TH MTN MAP: Mount Yeckel
USGS MAPS: Crooked Creek Pass, Mount Jackson

If you like to explore, variations on this branch route could keep you busy for days. This area is especially good for orienteering practice. You'll find a draconian lack of navigable ridges and valleys, and plenty of dense forest alternating with vast clearings.

ROUTE DESCRIPTION: To begin, climb Burnt Mountain (route 5.7). Remove your skins at the summit and enjoy a run NE off the summit into the sprawling (and somewhat confusing) meadows of Tellurium Park.

Ski to the area just W of the point 10,690 (you can see this from the summit of Burnt Mountain) and then to the north end of the clearing where three pack trails come together. Ski through timber NW to the next meadow (use the trail cut to avoid dense timber) and ski to the north end of this long clearing. For a good landmark use the "weird hole" in the middle of the meadow. Next, follow the pack trail N down into Slim Jim Gulch. Then take Slim Jim Gulch 1 1/4 miles down to the Burnt Mountain Road, where you follow the later part of 10th Mountain suggested route 5.2 up to the Harry Gates Hut. With adroit compass, altimeter, and map work you can take a shortcut directly to the Gates from the lower end of Slim Jim.

For a shorter return to the hut, use the pack trail (The Choker Cutoff) that circles the northwest slope of Burnt Mountain between 10,000 and 10,300 feet elevation. Follow Choker Cutoff to the Burnt Mountain ascent route, then ski down to the hut. Finding this trail can be hard, but it's easy to follow once you do.

SAFETY NOTES: Use proper avalanche safety procedures while skiing into Slim Jim Gulch, and off the summit of Burnt Mountain.

SUMMER: The network of trails in the Tellurium Park area are great for hiking and horses. Because of the close proximity of the Holy Cross Wilderness, mountain bikers should use routes closer to Lime Park.

Chapter 6 • Peter Estin Hut

Built in 1985, the Peter Estin Hut was the third publicly funded hut added to the 10th Mountain system. It is centered in a vast forested area with access to myriad trails, dirt roads, and one alpine ridge. The hut sits in a clearing

ELEVATION: 11,200 feet
COUNTY: Eagle
TEXT MAP: pp. 72-73, 100-101
10TH MTN MAP: Burnt Mt., N.Y. Mt.
USGS MAP: Crooked Creek Pass
TRAILHEADS: Sylvan Lake, Yeoman Park

on a timbered saddle, just northwest of Charles Peak (12,050 feet), with a clear view of the Elk and Williams mountains to the south.

If you have used other "standard" 10th Mountain huts, the Peter Estin will look familiar. It stands two stories high with a commodious deck jutting from the front door. Inside you'll find solar-powered electric lights, a gas stove, wood heat, and berths for 16 travelers. Plenty of windows face the south views.

In the past the Peter Estin Hut has been open in the summer. A call to 10th Mountain will get you the latest information concerning the current summer policy. Summer is a terrific season for enjoying this hut. Cyclists can use hundreds of miles of low-angled logging roads that surround the hut, and there are plenty of options for hikers and equestrians.

Building the Peter Estin Hut was a part of the trend by 10th Mountain to build huts closer to timber line, with access to terrain that varies from forest walks to technical climbing. To that end, alpine access from the Estin Hut is available via the Charles Ridge (route 6.8). For powder skiers, the face of Charles Ridge just above the hut is a fine playground with minimal avalanche danger. Terrain that's more radical is available outside the front door of the hut (see route 6.6). For ski-throughs use route 6.5 or 6.6 to the Harry Gates Hut, and route 6.2 or 6.3 to descend north into the Yeoman Park and Fulford area.

6.1

Sylvan Lake Trailhead — Peter Estin Hut via Crooked Creek Pass

DIFFICULTY: Intermediate
TIME: 11 hours up, 8 hours down
DISTANCE: 9 ½ miles
ELEVATION GAIN: 2,907 feet; elevation loss: 265 feet
10TH MTN MAP: Burnt Mountain
USGS MAP: Crooked Creek Pass

This 10th Mountain suggested route is a long trail that uses miles of popular snowmobile track. Thus, it might prove attractive after a new snow which could mean strenuous trailbreaking on a lesser used trail. For a less mechanized, shorter route to the hut use the Ironedge Trail (route 6.3).

Aerial view of the Peter Estin Hut from the southwest.

ROUTE DESCRIPTION: To begin, drive to the Sylvan Lake Trailhead. Start with cross country wax. From your parking place at snow closure, ski up the distinct snow-covered West Brush Creek road cut (also called the Eagle Road) around the north and east sides of the lake, then on up into the Brush Creek valley for 4 ¾ miles to Crooked Creek Pass. In detail: use your altimeter to identify the switchbacks at 9,220 feet and 9,260 feet, then the turn at 9,450 feet. After this turn, be extra careful to stay on the road as it climbs around a timbered ridge dividing Spine Creek from Brush Creek and then continues paralleling Brush Creek to Crooked Creek Pass (10,005 feet).

Now the real climbing begins (consider skins). Leave the West Brush Creek (Eagle) Road at the summit of the pass and turn NW (on the west side of an obvious fence) up a road cut that climbs just over ¼ mile to a switchback, then SE to another switchback, then around the west shoulder of point 11,087. The road, still an obvious cut, follows a long traverse on the north side of point 11,087, then drops 260 vertical feet to a saddle near the head of Spine Creek (10,700 feet).

Stay on the road from the saddle for another ⅛ mile NE to the switchback as shown on the USGS Crooked Creek Pass map. Leave the road here and climb E ¼ mile and 90 vertical feet to the top of the ridge separating Spine Creek from Little Lime Creek. Here your route converges with the Lime Ridge Trail (route 5.5) and continues N up a well-marked route through aspen and conifer, then a sparsely timbered logging area. Keep your eyes open for the interesting tree inscriptions on the aspen trees along the trail.

Like many of the other huts, the Peter Estin is slightly hidden from the trail, and you can ski past it if you are not paying attention. To prevent this mistake, as you ski through the forest use your altimeter and map to identify the three trail confluence that you hit at a broad saddle (Hat Creek Saddle) just west of the hut. Swing E at the saddle, and when you break through a grove of pines the hut will be in front of you. Sniffing for wood smoke can help too, but your compass is more reliable.

REVERSE ROUTE DESCRIPTION: Follow route 6.4 to Crooked Creek Pass, where you intersect the Eagle Road. Turn right (NW) onto the Eagle Road and follow it down the Brush Creek valley 4 ¾ miles to the Sylvan Lake Trailhead.

SAFETY NOTES: Take care with route finding in Spine Creek, since the trail only uses the upper part of the drainage.

SUMMER: All these roads make fine equestrian, bicycle, and hiking routes.

6.2

Yeoman Park Trailhead — Peter Estin Hut via Hat Creek

DIFFICULTY: Intermediate
TIME: 8 hours up, 6 hours down
DISTANCE: 7 1/2 miles
ELEVATION GAIN: 2,140 feet
10TH MTN MAP: New York Mountain
USGS MAPS: Fulford, Meredith

As an ascent route many skiers will find this 10th Mountain suggested route to be quite tedious, but it is a perfect descent for those with minimal ski skills. The steeper alternative is the Ironedge Trail (route 6.3).

ROUTE DESCRIPTION: To ski the Hat Creek route, begin at the Yeoman Park Trailhead. Start with cross country wax but keep your skins handy. From your parking spot, carefully identify the start of the Hat Creek Road. It begins just W of the actual campground and follows a distinct road cut up a southeast climbing traverse. Follow the road to the first switchback and continue climbing NW through several more switchbacks. Stay on the road; at 9,400 feet you'll swing S into the Hat Creek drainage.

Once in Hat Creek, the route continues to be obvious and well marked. Basically, you stay on the main logging road as it parallels Hat Creek. The only deviation from the creek takes some switchbacks starting at 9,800 feet elevation. At a 10,820-foot saddle (Ironedge Saddle) at the head of the Hat Creek drainage, the logging road makes a turn to the S. Leave the road here, ski several hundred feet farther E, and intersect the continuation of the Ironedge Trail that 10th Mountain has marked. Climb this trail 3/4 mile SE up through timber to the Peter Estin Hut. This section of trail is less obvious than the logging roads, so pay attention.

REVERSE ROUTE DESCRIPTION: For the reverse, ski fifty feet W of the hut, then N downhill through timber to the 10,820-foot saddle (Ironedge Saddle). Though this route is marked by 10th Mountain, the pull of cutting turns could lead you past the saddle and down the Ironedge Trail (route 6.3). This will be fine for good skiers, since in this case "all roads lead to Rome". Intermediate skiers, however, should make an effort to stay in Hat Creek — the icy toboggan run downhills on the Ironedge require legs of steel and an edge of courage.

SAFETY NOTES: This is a very safe, mellow route. Beware of "blue diamond dependency", or you could end up in the Ironedge treatment center.

SUMMER: The Hat Creek Road is a fine bicycle, equestrian, and hiking route. Summer users should use the road all the way to Hat Creek Saddle, as the 10th Mountain route up from Ironedge Saddle does not follow a summer path — it is just a marked route through the forest.

6.3

Yeoman Park Trailhead — Peter Estin Hut via Ironedge Trail

DIFFICULTY: Intermediate (advanced for descent)
TIME: 6 hours up, 4 hours down
DISTANCE: 4 1/2 miles
ELEVATION GAIN: 2,140 feet
10TH MTN MAP: New York Mountain
USGS MAPS: Fulford, Crooked Creek Pass

This 10th Mountain suggested route follows a fine single track trail that is closed to snowmobiles. It is an efficient ascent route, but can be a hairy downhill. Those with minimal turn skill should consider descending Hat Creek (route 6.2).

ROUTE DESCRIPTION: From the Yeoman Park Trailhead ski (or walk depending on snow cover) N back across the bridge over East Brush Creek, then turn right (E) onto the East Brush Creek Road. The first part of this route uses the snow-covered East Brush Creek Road for 1 1/2 miles to roads end at Fulford Cave Campground. As you ski up the road, you'll pass two left turns onto other 10th Mountain suggested trails: the Fulford Road (route 7.1) at just under 1/2 mile and the Newcomer Spring Trail (route 7.2) after another 3/4 mile at 9,280 feet. Be sure not to turn onto these trails.

At Fulford Cave Campground swing around the east end of a small lake, then back W for a few hundred feet to a distinct trail cut that heads through private property. Stay on the trail as it leads past several buildings and begins to climb — and climb. The switchbacks start at 9,560 feet, and they keep you breathing hard to the Ironedge Saddle at 10,820 feet.

Take care at Ironedge Saddle to identify the marked 10th Mountain suggested route that leads SE then S up through timber to the Peter Estin Hut. There is the possibility of confusion leading you on to the Hat Creek Road, then up to Hat Creek Saddle (see map in text). If this happens, just ski E to the hut from Hat Creek Saddle. To prevent confusion, use your compass at Ironedge Saddle.

REVERSE ROUTE DESCRIPTION: To descend the Ironedge Trail, ski fifty feet W of the Peter Estin Hut, then take care to turn N onto the 10th

Mountain suggested route down through timber to the Ironedge Saddle. Some map work in the hut will help you get a good start. From the Ironedge Saddle ski the fall line for a short distance to a dropping traverse to the left. This traverse leads to the famous Ironedge switchbacks.

SAFETY NOTES: There is no slide danger here. Ski in control.

SUMMER: The Ironedge Trail is a good horse and hike route. Expert mountain bike riders love it as a descent route, but find it an impossible ascent. Cyclists should use Hat Creek to gain their vertical. A good loop goes up Hat Creek, then down the Ironedge.

6.4
Peter Estin Hut to Harry Gates Hut via Crooked Creek Pass

DIFFICULTY: Intermediate
TIME: 7 hours
DISTANCE: 9 1/2 miles
ELEVATION GAIN: 775 feet; elevation loss: 2,275 feet
10TH MTN MAP: Burnt Mountain
USGS MAP: Crooked Creek Pass

This 10th Mountain suggested route wanders, but it is an excellent choice if you prefer mellow downhills. Leave your skins in your pack and use cross country wax.

ROUTE DESCRIPTION: Get out your map and compass while you're still in the hut, review this route, and remember to calibrate your altimeter. From the front steps of the Peter Estin Hut ski W about 600 feet to Hat Creek Saddle. From Hat Creek Saddle travel S down through a sparsely timbered logging area, then through dense conifer and aspen. At 10,850 feet take a crucial right (W) turn into the Spine Creek drainage and drop 90 vertical feet to the Spine Creek logging road (10,760 feet) at the head of the Spine Creek drainage.

Take care here as the route follows the logging road which, instead of descending the drainage, takes a climbing traverse W along the south side of the drainage. The climb takes you 3/4 mile to 10,965 feet where the road begins to drop, then takes an obvious left (S) turn, and drops through two switchbacks to Crooked Creek Pass. From here follow route 5.3 to the Harry Gates Hut.

SAFETY NOTES: Take care with route finding so that you drop into Spine Creek, and be sure to find the logging road out of Spine Creek, since an inadvertent descent of Spine Creek will place you far down the Brush Creek Road on the wrong side of Crooked Creek Pass

SUMMER: Hikers, bikers, and horseback riders can use this route. At the head of Spine Creek deviate from the 10th Mountain suggested route and use the logging road and trail as marked on the USGS Crooked Creek Pass map.

6.5

Peter Estin Hut to Harry Gates Hut via Lime Ridge Trail

DIFFICULTY: Intermediate
TIME: 6 hours
DISTANCE: 7 miles
ELEVATION GAIN: 630 feet; elevation loss: 2,130 feet
10TH MTN MAP: Burnt Mountain
USGS MAP: Crooked Creek Pass

This is certainly the most efficient 10th Mountain suggested route between the Peter Estin Hut and Harry Gates Hut. It has some fast downhill sections, so be sure you can push a strong snowplow. The first half of the route descends the ridge separating Little Lime Creek from Middle Creek. Keep this in mind while navigating.

ROUTE DESCRIPTION: While still inside the hut, enjoy a cup of tea while you do a map check and set your altimeter. Keep your skins in your pack. From the front steps of the Peter Estin Hut ski W about 600 feet to Hat Creek Saddle. From Hat Creek Saddle travel S down through a sparsely timbered logging area, past the right turn (route 6.4) into Spine Creek, and into the trees on the east side of the ridge (10,845 feet). Continue down the ridge and around one switchback to a flat area at 10,200 feet. Just below the switchback enjoy the old inscriptions on the mature aspen trees.

From the flat area, continue S ¼ mile down the ridge, through the dense evergreens of Sherwood Forest, and to the meadows at 10,150 feet. Ski the marked trail as it uses intermittent clearings to descend the ridge crest down to the end of the ridge. Here, instead of dropping off the steep end of the ridge, the trail switchbacks left (N) and takes a descending traverse ¼ mile to a crossing of Little Lime Creek at 9,700 feet.

Ski ½ mile down the east side of Little Lime Creek, cross the east fork of Little Lime Creek, then begin a gradual climb S then W 1 mile to an indistinct jeep trail on top of the ridge. Descend the jeep trail ¾ mile SW along the ridge crest, then drop S into Lime Park, and continue S across Lime Park to the bridge crossing Lime Creek at 9,190 feet. The route across

Lime Park follows dirt roads. These are usually obscured by the snow cover, but the junctions are well signed and several fence breaks show where the road goes.

Lime Park can be a sublime place for ski touring, with Avalanche Peak looming to the east, and the sculpted snowscape of the park. But the place is so vast that navigating in poor visibility can be a nightmare. The danger is that you'll miss the crossing of Lime Creek and descend into Lime Creek Canyon, a narrow trap. You must find the bridge crossing Lime Creek at 9,190 feet, and the only way to do that in a whiteout is with compass and altimeter, and perhaps the occasional blue diamond.

From the bridge over Lime Creek follow the snow-covered Burnt Mountain Road as it climbs E than S up to a band of timber, then breaks out into another open area at Slim Jim Gulch. Stay on the road and continue S ¾ mile to 9,566 feet on the Burnt Mountain Road. Leave the road here. Take a left (E) turn and climb a hill ¼ mile NE to the Harry Gates Hut. You can't see the hut when you turn from the road — it comes into sight when you're about halfway up the hill. This climb is too short to warrant skins, but you may have to use a few herringbone steps.

SAFETY NOTES: Ski in control on the downhills. Pay attention to route finding in Lime Park. Be courteous to snowmobiles in Lime Park and they will return in-kind.

SUMMER: The Lime Ridge portion of this route is only a marked route, there is no real path. Thus, hikers and equestrians should consider the pack trail in the Little Lime Creek drainage (see route 6.6). The roads in Lime Park are fine for all activities.

6.6
Peter Estin Hut to Harry Gates Hut via Lime Drainage Trail

DIFFICULTY: Advanced
TIME: 5 ½ hours
DISTANCE: 6 ¼ miles
ELEVATION GAIN: 630 feet; elevation loss: 2,130 feet
10TH MTN MAP: Burnt Mountain
USGS MAP: Crooked Creek Pass

This alternate route hits some good downhill skiing and cuts ¾ mile off the Lime Ridge Trail (route 6.5). Because it is unmarked and has a a small amount of potential slide danger, only advanced skiers should use this route.

Since you are going cold turkey from "blue diamond dependency", you should be extra sure to carry—and know how to use—your map, compass, and altimeter.

ROUTE DESCRIPTION: The best way to begin is by making turns down the bowl that starts just a few feet S of the hut. There can be avalanche danger here, so determine the conditions before you jump in, and use proper procedure while skiing.

To get the best ski line, stay a bit W of the bowl proper and ski a small ridge S to an opening in the creek bottom (10,560 feet). From here you can contour SE to the large open slope E of the creek. Work this slope, then traverse S to another smaller bowl. At 10,000 feet cross the creek and descend the west side of the creek to 9,850 feet, then intersect route 6.5 at the crossing of Little Lime Creek. Follow route 6.5 to the Harry Gates Hut.

SAFETY NOTES: For this route you should be skilled in avalanche hazard guesswork, navigation, and downhill skiing. Any slide danger can be avoided by skiing through the trees on either side of the open areas.

SUMMER: Hikers and horses can use the pack trail that follows Little Lime Creek. Cyclists will find better riding on the dirt roads in the area.

6.7

Peter Estin Hut to Polar Star Inn

DIFFICULTY: Intermediate (difficult downhill)
TIME: 9 hours (Ironedge Trail)
DISTANCE: 8 1⁄4 miles (Ironedge Trail)
ELEVATION GAIN: 1,900 feet; elevation loss: 2,060 feet
10TH MTN MAP: New York Mountain
USGS MAPS: Crooked Creek Pass, Fulford

Since the routes from the Peter Estin hut to the Polar Star Inn pass through or close to the Yeoman Park Trailhead, they are detailed in other route descriptions and only referenced here.

ROUTE DESCRIPTION: To travel from the Peter Estin Hut to the Polar Star Inn you can pick from several routes down into the East Brush Creek drainage, and several that climb out of the drainage and N to the Inn. The most direct route down from the Peter Estin Hut is the Ironedge Trail (route 6.3). Skiers with minimal downhill skills should consider using Hat Creek (route 6.2). Hat Creek adds about 4 miles (and several hours) to the trip.

You have two choices for the climb up from East Brush Creek to the Inn. If you're coming from Hat Creek, use the Fulford Road route (route 7.1). If you skied the Ironedge, ascend the Newcomer Spring route (route 7.2). Remember that whatever your route, this is a long trip; start early. For safety and summer notes, see the routes referenced above.

6.8

Charles Peak and Fools Peak from the Peter Estin Hut

DIFFICULTY: Intermediate to expert
TIME: Several hours to a full day round trip
DISTANCE: Charles Peak, 1 ½ miles round trip
Fools Peak, 6 ¼ miles round trip

ELEVATION GAIN: Charles Peak, 900 feet round trip; Fools Peak, 2,750 feet round trip
10TH MTN MAP: New York Mountain
USGS MAPS: Crooked Creek Pass, Mount Jackson

If you want a branch route that climbs to alpine terrain from the Peter Estin Hut, you only have one choice—the Charles Ridge. Beginning at Charles Peak E of the Estin Hut and extending 4 miles to Eagle Peak, this ridge probes the Holy Cross Mountains where 14,005-foot Mount of the Holy Cross lords over scores of 12,000- and 13,000-foot peaks. In winter conditions intermediate skiers should venture no farther than Charles Peak. Here you'll find good skiing from the summit back towards the hut, and a worthy view. Advanced skiers can climb Fools Peak, and expert mountaineers can attempt a long ridge run to Eagle Peak.

ROUTE DESCRIPTION: To reach the summit of Charles Peak climb NE from the Peter Estin Hut into a clearing where you'll usually find some exuberant ski tracks—and skiers. Climb the clearing to the ridge, then follow the ridge SE to the summit. For your descent you can stick to the ridge then ski the clearing, or ski the open area W of the summit down to treeline, then traverse to the aforementioned clearing.

The summit of Fools Peak is a worthy goal, but requires advanced skill in all aspects of winter mountaineering. Parties on this climb should carry avalanche rescue beacons. The route follows the Charles Ridge to the 12,100-foot saddle just W of the Fools Peak summit. From the saddle you cut a short traverse, then climb the west face to the summit, sticking to the ridge to your left (as much as you can) to lessen avalanche exposure. Return via the same route.

Skiing Charles Peak; Lime Park in the background.

SAFETY NOTES: There is a great deal of slide terrain on the sides of Charles Ridge. While on the ridge it may take a bit of extra effort to stay off the avalanche slopes on the ridge sides, especially while negotiating point 11,905. Remember that you are traveling above timber line in alpine conditions different than those you deal with down in the woods. Carry full bivouac gear and ski conservatively.

SUMMER: Charles Ridge is a wonderful alpine hike. You should have mountaineering skills to wander beyond Fools Peak.

Chapter 7 • Polar Star Inn

The Polar Star Inn is a privately owned back-country lodge located on 10th Mountain suggested routes, just below timber line on the west side of New York Mountain. The Inn, which sleeps 17, is booked by 10th Mountain.

ELEVATION: 11,040 feet
COUNTY: Eagle
TEXT MAP: pp. 100-101
10TH MTN MAP: New York Mountain
USGS MAP: Fulford
TRAILHEADS: Yeoman Park, West Lake Creek

The Polar Star Inn is a tall-standing structure with a big deck that looks west over the Colorado Plateau — a sunset watcher's paradise. There are 5 private bedrooms, and running water that makes kitchen work a snap. The Polar Star has no showers, but you can get clean in the wood-heated sauna. The toilet is the traditional outhouse. The Inn was built in 1987.

Open year-round, the Polar Star provides all-season access to a huge area of National Forest, including the Holy Cross Wilderness. Outside the wilderness you'll find superb mountain bike riding on jeep trails and unimproved roads. One popular bike trail is the old Fulford Road that descends from the west end of Fulford down to East Brush Creek. Other good rides follow the jeep trail from Dubach Meadows out into the Bumpity Park area. If you're fit, you can ride from Bumpity Park all the way to Eagle. Hikers and equestrians can also find options in all directions.

Skiers can take their pick of trails to and from the Inn, as well as several fine branch routes. For starters, you'll find superb tree skiing just out the

door of the hut. For advanced skiers, a short easterly climb leads above timber line to the west slopes of New York Mountain (route 7.5). From there take your choice of bowls and steep gullies. Intermediate backcountry skiers can also climb New York Mountain, then use a low-angled route for descent.

If you plan a ski-through to the north from the Polar Star, be aware that you'll have to use a car shuttle to get from the West Lake Creek Trailhead to the next part of 10th Mountain suggested route (Chapters 8 to 13). More huts and trails are planed to help connect through this section.

7.1

Yeoman Park Trailhead — Polar Star Inn via Fulford Road

DIFFICULTY: Intermediate
TIME: 5 hours up
DISTANCE: 6 1/4 miles
ELEVATION GAIN: 2,080 feet; elevation loss: 100 feet
10TH MTN MAP: New York Mountain
USGS MAP: Fulford

This 10th Mountain suggested route follows distinct road cuts and well-marked trails. It is heavily traveled by snowmobiles. Thus, the foot-travel-only Newcomer Spring route (route 7.2) might be a more attractive alternative for skiers.

ROUTE DESCRIPTION: From Yeoman Park Campground ski or walk (depending on snow cover) back N across the bridge and turn right onto the East Brush Creek Road. Follow the obvious road cut up the valley for just under 1/2 mile and make a hard left turn on to the well-signed Fulford Road. Follow the Fulford Road as it climbs NW then N around a shoulder, then winds up through superb forest via several switchbacks to McGinley Gulch. Stay on the road from McGinley Gulch as it climbs NW 1/4 mile, then turns N around another shoulder, then drops 3/4 mile and 100 vertical feet to cross Nolan Creek (10,060 feet) just E of the small group of buildings known as Fulford.

Just after you cross the bridge over Nolan Creek, turn right on another snow-covered road leading towards Upper Town and ski 1/8 mile to a left (N) turn onto a marked 10th Mountain trail. If you had your nose to the grindstone on the roads to this point, look up. This section does not follow a snow-covered road, so it requires more attention. Climb 1 mile up 5 switchbacks to the New York Mountain jeep trail (10,520 feet). Take a right on the snow-covered jeep trail and follow it as it climbs 1/2 mile to 10,830 feet. Leave the jeep trail here and continue NE on a 10th Mountain marked trail 1/2 mile to the Polar Star Inn.

REVERSE ROUTE DESCRIPTION: From the front of the Polar Star Inn, carefully locate the 10th Mountain marked trail leading SW down the mountain in a dropping traverse. At 1/2 mile (10,830 feet) the trail intersects the New York Mountain jeep trail. Continue down the jeep trail 1/2

Bellyache Mountain

West Lake Creek Trailhead
9.220

1.00 miles to West Lake Creek
6.00 miles to Polar Star Inn

2.42 miles to West Lake Creek
4.58 miles to Polar Star Inn

Card Creek

7.3

× 9991.9
3863

Elk Park

× 9890
3074

Squaw Creek

3.88 miles to West Lake Creek
3.11 miles to Polar Star Inn

2.65 miles to Polar Star Inn
4.35 miles to West Lake Creek

2.11 miles to Polar Star Inn
4.89 miles to West Lake Creek

1.00 miles to Polar Star Inn
6.00 miles to West Lake Creek

7.3
7.6

Poison Gl.

Big Park

Dry Gulch

7.6

WHITE RIVER
NATIONAL FOREST

HOLY CROSS WILDERNESS

Snowslide
Park

JEEP

TRAIL

Bowman Gulch

Dubach
Meadows

Devils Canyon

Porphyry
Mountain

Triangle
Park

Willow
Park

SALT CREEK TRAIL

JEEP

JEEP

To Eagle

10th Mountain Hut & Trail System

Scale 1 : 24,000

SCALE IN MILES

0   .25   .50   .75   1

MN 12°

Hut   ●
Trailhead   ★

Trails are marked by blue diamonds, except in
wilderness areas where trails are marked by tree blazes.
This map is not a substitute for good route finding skills;
it is just an aid to help locate routes.
These are suggested routes only.
Trails are not groomed and their exact location may vary.

© 1989 · 10th Mountain Trail Association

10th Mountain Trail is located in the White River
and San Isabel National Forests.
Taylor sigheen.net with the Forest Service, USDA

Eagle Peak

Gold Dust Peak

Pools Peak

Negro Basin

Gold Dust Basin

New York Mountain

New York Mountain

FULFORD GROUSE MOUNTAIN
CROOKED-CREEK PASS
MOUNT JACKSON

Craig Peak

Charles Peak

Ironedge Trail

Hat Creek

7.1

Yeoman Trailhead
9,060'

1.70 miles to Yeoman Park
4.55 miles to Polar Star Inn

6.7
7.2
7.4

0.40 miles to Yeoman Park
1.90 miles to Fulford Cave
Campground

6.7
7.2
7.4

3.57 miles to Polar Star Inn
4.64 miles to Peter Estin Hut

3.40 miles to Yeoman Park
4.81 miles to Peter Estin Hut

1.40 miles to Yeoman Park
3.00 miles to Peter Estin Hut
5.21 miles to Polar Star Inn

2.30 miles to Yeoman Park
5.02 miles to Peter Estin Hut

6.3
6.7
7.4

6.2

5.4
6.1
6.4

0.72 miles to Peter Estin Hut
6.60 miles to Yeoman Park via Hat Creek Road
7.49 miles to Polar Star Inn

Peter Estin Hut
11,200'

0.77 miles to Peter Estin Hut
3.40 miles to Crooked Creek Pass
6.22 miles to Harry Gates Hut

6.8

5.6
6.6

5.5
6.5

To Lime Park — continued on pp. 72-73

Crooked Creek Pass

mile (to 10,520 feet) and turn S off the jeep trail. If you want the quickest downhill, take care not to miss this turn; if you want an easier downhill you can stay on the jeep trail and follow it to the Fulford Road, which you then ski SE to intersect the 10th Mountain suggested route near Fulford.

After you turn off the jeep trail, ski five fast switchbacks (experts can cut some of these) down to Upper Town, then W ⅛ mile down a snow-covered road to intersect the Fulford Road. Turn left (SW) onto the Fulford Road and ski the distinct, snow-covered Fulford Road 4 ⅛ miles to the Yeoman Park Trailhead.

SAFETY NOTES: There is no avalanche danger on this route. Take care while tree skiing down to Upper Town.

SUMMER: The roads on this route make for fine mountain biking. To reach the Polar Star Inn by bicycle or car, simply stay on the Fulford Road past Fulford. You can either stay on the Fulford Road as it traverses through Triangle Creek then swings around and climbs New York Mountain, or you can use the New York Mountain jeep trail. Both routes are well rendered on the USGS Fulford map. There is no sign at the turn-off from the main road to the Polar Star Inn. The turn-off is usually closed with a cable gate.

7.2

Yeoman Park Trailhead — Polar Star Inn via Newcomer Spring

DIFFICULTY: Intermediate
TIME: 4 ¾ hours up, 3 hours down
DISTANCE: 6 miles
ELEVATION GAIN: 2,140 feet; elevation loss: 160 feet
10TH MTN MAP: New York Mountain
USGS MAPS: Crooked Creek Pass, Fulford

Pick this 10th Mountain suggested route for a more serene wilderness experience. It avoids snowmobile trails and climbs more efficiently than other routes which stick to the roads. The trail is slightly more difficult to find than route 7.1.

ROUTE DESCRIPTION: From the Yeoman Park Trailhead, ski (or walk depending on snow cover) up the main road on the north side of the East Brush Creek valley. At just under ½ mile, while still in Yeoman Park, you'll come to the distinct switchback left (NW) onto the Fulford Road. Do not make this turn, instead continue another ¾ mile to 9,280 feet. At this point, look carefully on the left for a 10th Mountain marked trail. Turn left onto the trail (put your skins on) and follow it as it climbs a few hundred feet E (paralleling the road below), then switchbacks left (NW).

Stay on the trail as it makes a climbing traverse to 9,520 feet, switchbacks right, and climbs to 10,000 feet. The trail eases off here, gradually climbs N, makes a long contour around a shoulder, then drops about 80 vertical feet to Nolan Creek at 10,180 feet. Cross Nolan Creek, then follow the trail as it winds N ¾ mile to Upper Town (10,060 feet), where you take the right (N) turn onto the 10th Mountain marked route. See route 7.1 for the remainder of the route from Upper Town to the Polar Star Inn.

REVERSE ROUTE DESCRIPTION: To reverse the route, follow 7.1 to Upper Town. Take care in Upper Town to turn left (E) off 7.1 onto a well-marked 10th Mountain trail that leads several hundred feet, crosses White Quail Gulch, then turns south and leads you across Nolan Creek. From here stay on the trail as it winds through beautiful forest, then drops down several switchbacks into East Brush Creek. Here the main road leads right (W) down the valley to Yeoman Park Trailhead, or up the valley to the Ironedge Trail (see route 6.3).

SAFETY NOTES: There is no slide danger on this route. Don't tangle with any aspens on the downhills and watch your feet at the stream crossings.

SUMMER: Hikers and horse people should check this one out. Cyclists should use the roads in route 7.1.

7.3

West Lake Creek Trailhead — Polar Star Inn

DIFFICULTY:
TIME: 8 ½ hours up
DISTANCE: 7 miles
ELEVATION GAIN: 3,000 feet; elevation loss: 180 feet
10TH MTN MAP: New York Mountain
USGS MAPS: Grouse Mountain, Fulford

This fine wilderness ski tour is a 10th Mountain suggested route. Remember that a large chunk of the trail is in designated wilderness, and thus marked with tree blazes instead of the ubiquitous blue diamonds.

ROUTE DESCRIPTION: The first portion of this trip makes several critical turns. From the West Lake Creek Trailhead ski a snow-covered road up the east side of Card Creek. Stay on the road as it crosses Card Creek at ¼ mile, then follows the west side of Card Creek another ¾ mile to another crossing (8,560 feet). Just past this crossing, it is critical to swing back right (SW) to stay in the Card Creek drainage. From here the snow-covered jeep trail climbs the east side of the drainage for 1 ¼ miles to another critical junction at 9,370 feet.

Here you turn right (SW) off the jeep trail onto the Card Creek Springs foot trail. Follow this trail S then W past Card Creek Springs (not that obvious), then up 500 vertical feet via 4 switchbacks to Card Creek Saddle (9,980 feet). From the saddle, follow the 10th Mountain marked trail as it drops along the New England Traverse W then NW into the Squaw Creek drainage to 9,800 feet. Stay on the trail as it takes a gradually climbing traverse ½ mile, crosses Squaw Creek, then follows the Squaw Creek drainage (crosses creek several more times) up to nondescript Squaw Creek Saddle (wilderness boundary) at the head of the drainage (10,620 feet). The trail passes slightly to the E of the low point in the saddle. From Squaw Creek Saddle follow the 10th Mountain marked trail one more mile SE to the Polar Star Inn. In stormy weather visibility may be poor above the saddle, so take a compass and altimeter reading near the saddle.

REVERSE ROUTE DESCRIPTION: The reverse of this route is a little easier because once you're at Card Creek Saddle, Card Creek leads you down to the West Lake Creek Trailhead, even if you loose the trail markers. The main thing to remember is that this trip uses two drainages and that you have to switch at the proper point. To do this, take care to reach Squaw

Creek Saddle from the Polar Star Inn (use your compass). Drop N from Squaw Creek Saddle down Squaw Creek to 9,840 feet. Turn NW then E here, drop a bit more, then take a climbing traverse to Card Creek Saddle.

SAFETY NOTES: This trip is basically a walk through the forest, so there is no slide danger. Since it does switch drainages, take care with route finding to hedge against the dire consequences of trail marker addiction.

SUMMER: This route makes a fine hike and horseback ride. If you like mountain biking, you'll find some good riding up to the wilderness boundary from the West Lake Creek Trailhead, but remember that even possessing a bicycle in the wilderness is a crime punishable by death (unless your bike is disguised as a horse).

7.4

Polar Star Inn to Peter Estin Hut via Ironedge Trail

DIFFICULTY: Intermediate
TIME: 9 hours
DISTANCE: 8 ¼ miles
ELEVATION GAIN: 1,920 feet; elevation loss: 1760 feet
10TH MTN MAP: New York Mountain
USGS MAPS: Fulford, Crooked Creek Pass

This is the only efficient ski route from the Polar Star Inn to the Peter Estin Hut. Even so, it is a long trail which requires many route-finding decisions. The route is described in detail under other referenced routes.

ROUTE DESCRIPTION: First, pick a route from the Polar Star Inn down into the East Brush Creek drainage. The Newcomer Spring route (reverse route 7.2) is the most direct. Once on the snow-covered East Brush Creek Road, use the Ironedge Trail (route 6.3) to ascend to the Peter Estin Hut.

SAFETY NOTES: Get an early start for this long route. See referenced routes for other safety suggestions.

SUMMER: To descend from the Polar Star Inn to the East Brush Creek drainage, cyclists should use the dirt roads via Fulford. Hikers and equestrians can use any number of trails, including the Newcomer Spring route (7.2). The Ironedge Trail is a good uphill horse and hike route, but too steep for bicycle travel. Cyclists should use the Hat Creek Road (route 6.2) to ascend to the Peter Estin Hut.

7.5

New York Mountain from Polar Star Inn

DIFFICULTY: Intermediate to Advanced
TIME: Easily a half day trip; a full day for more skiing
DISTANCE: About 2 miles round trip
ELEVATION GAIN: 1,380 feet round trip
10TH MTN MAP: New York Mountain
USGS MAPS: Fulford, Grouse Mountain

This popular summit climb gives you some honest mountain skiing and good views. Downhillers will like the turn options, but this terrain is above timber line so be ready for dreaded trap crust.

ROUTE DESCRIPTION: The route is simple. Put your skins on at the Polar Star Inn, climb SE to timber line, then choose a route that intersects New York Mountain's north ridge. Follow the ridge to the summit. You'll want climbing skins for this route, and you'll probably end up walking up wind-scoured areas. Possible downhill skiing varies with snow cover. In general, try the west face (open areas drop down into the trees) or the upper part of White Quail Gulch.

SAFETY NOTES: Suddenly, this route takes you into alpine regions above timber line — a different environment than the forest below. Visibility can deteriorate rapidly and snow conditions can make downhill skiing all but impossible. There is steep avalanche terrain on the east side of the north and south summit ridges, and slide potential in upper White Quail Gulch. Also, given a load of extremely unstable snow, any of the slopes on New York Mountain could avalanche. Beware of cornices on all ridges.

SUMMER: This summit is a fine goal for a hike. The trail is too steep and rocky for bicycles and horses.

7.6

Bellyache Mountain from Polar Star Inn

DIFFICULTY: Advanced
TIME: 12 hours or overnight round trip
DISTANCE: 14 miles round trip
ELEVATION GAIN: 1,500 feet round trip
10TH MTN MAP: New York Mountain
USGS MAP: Fulford

If you have less interest in downhill turns and a strong desire to cover the country, consider this trip. It is seldom skied, long, and intricate, but covers some pleasing terrain. If it sounds too long for you, remember that the return uses the same route, so just plan a closer destination.

ROUTE DESCRIPTION: To begin, ski from the Polar Star on the marked 10th Mountain suggested route down Squaw Creek (reverse route 7.3). Use your map and altimeter; at 9,960 feet in Squaw Creek leave the 10th Mountain route and continue down the west side of Squaw Creek to a gulch at 9,700 feet. Follow a road cut as it contours through the gulch, then gradually climbs and contours N then W around a shoulder, then drops 140 vertical feet into a saddle (9,590 feet) on Bellyache Ridge.

Bellyache Ridge is a broad, timbered, flat-topped ridge with lots of parks and good views. Using your map, compass, and altimeter, stick to the general route of the road marked on the USGS Fulford map. It gradually descends through timber and clearings to Big Park, then climbs 120 vertical feet back up into the large parks on top of Bellyache Mountain. This is a good final goal for the trip, as the trail past here looses altitude rapidly and would add too much time to your return. To reverse the route, follow your tracks back to the Polar Star Inn. Allow time for the climb back up Squaw Creek.

SAFETY NOTES: There is one critical consideration for success on this route — navigation. Be sure your party includes at least one expert orienteer. Since the route is so long, don't skimp on emergency bivouac gear.

SUMMER: The road on Bellyache Mountain provides terrific cycling, but getting there can be a formidable challenge. The problem is that the connecting route from the Polar Star, the Squaw Creek Trail, is in designated wilderness and thus closed to bicycles. Instead, you have to follow the roads on Logged Off Mountain as far N as you can, then, staying just W of the wilderness boundary, shoulder your bike and bushwhack down to the Bellyache Mountain Road. Since the bushwhack would be an uphill grunt on your return, you should consider riding all the way to Eagle or Edwards (be sure to carry the Seven Hermits and Wolcott USGS 7.5 minute maps if you take that option).

Chapter 8 • Shrine Mountain Inn

While still located far enough from paved roads to maintain a backcountry mood, the Shrine Mountain Inn is the easiest 10th Mountain "ski-in" accommodation to access, being just 2 ⅓ miles from Vail Pass Trailhead. The Inn consists of two

ELEVATION:	11,209 feet
COUNTY:	Summit
TEXT MAP:	pp. 110-111
10TH MTN MAP:	Resolution Mountain
USGS MAP:	Vail Pass
TRAILHEADS:	Vail Pass, Vail Trailhead for Commando Run, Red Cliff

privately owned cabins that sleep a total of 18 people. Most amenities are available: kitchen, hot and cold running water, showers, lights, and sauna. You bring your own sleeping bag or rent bedding and a towel. Catered meals are available if arranged in advance. The Inn is booked through 10th Mountain.

The Shrine Mountain Inn is open all year. In the summer, there is fine cycling, horseback riding, and cycling surrounding the Inn. The Shrine Pass dirt road (see route 8.3) is a popular bicycle cruise and a nice auto tour as well. Cyclists, hikers, and equestrians who want less auto dust can follow the Commando Run trail (route 8.2) to Vail. This is also a popular ski route in either direction.

WARREN OHLRICH

For ski-throughs, use the Shrine Mountain Ridge (route 8.4) for the fastest route to the Fowler/Hilliard Hut, or Shrine Pass (route 8.3) to get to Red Cliff. If you want to stay for a few nights and ski, cut some turns in the Black Lake Glades (route 8.6), or take a scenic tour up on Shrine Mountain (route 8.4). For regional skiing, you can also connect with the Copper Mountain Resort by using a ski trail that parallels I-70. Huts in this area are also being planned by Summit County Huts and Trails. You can reserve lodging in Red Cliff through 10th Mountain.

8.1

Vail Pass Trailhead — Shrine Mountain Inn

DIFFICULTY: Novice
TIME: 2 hours up, 1 hour down
DISTANCE: 2 ¾ miles
ELEVATION GAIN: 666 feet; elevation loss: 67 feet
10TH MTN MAP: Resolution Mountain
USGS MAP: Vail Pass

This is the shortest trailhead to hut route in the 10th Mountain system. Heavy use of the trail by snowmobiles and skier is a mixed blessing. The route is almost always packed out, but there can be hundreds of trails leading in all directions. Even though it looks simple, make a few map checks just to be sure. This is a 10th Mountain suggested route.

ROUTE DESCRIPTION: From the Vail Pass Trailhead ski SW on the snow-covered Shrine Pass Road. At ⅛ mile, swing N on a switchback, ski ¼ mile to another switchback (10,720 feet), then ski SW and W as the road parallels West Tenmile Creek while climbing up the ridge that forms the north side of the drainage. After a long ⅞ mile climbing traverse, the road leads to an 11,156-foot saddle on the ridge. This has been mistaken by many to be Shrine Pass, as it is a pass of sorts. Enjoy the view at the saddle (you can see Shrine Mountain Inn from here if you look sharp), but take care to follow the snow-covered Shrine Pass Road as it stays on the south side of the ridge and gradually drops ¾ mile NW to the real Shrine Pass. Shrine Pass is named for it's views of Mount of the Holy Cross which rises to the west. Holy Cross is famed for several snowfields on the north face that sometimes look like a Christian cross.

The pass looks more like a large park than the classic "pass summit" that most people are familiar with. Nevertheless, it is the divide between the Turkey Creek and West Tenmile Creek drainages. On Shrine Pass take care not to ski too far NW. Look for a White River National Forest sign. Ski W from this sign, several hundred yards across a clear area, and enter a

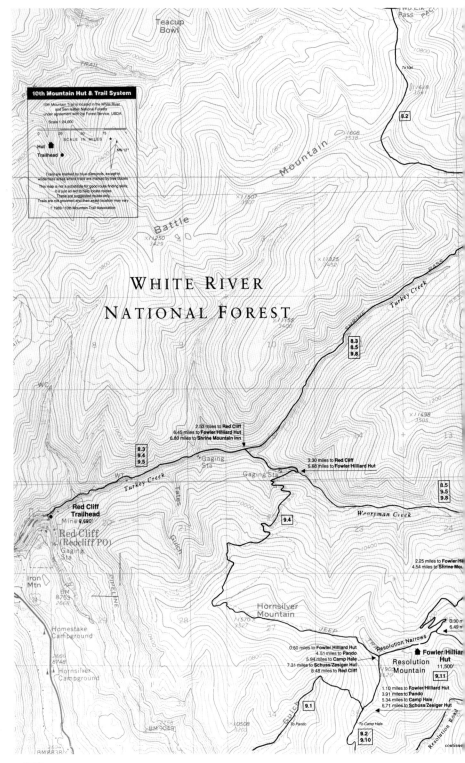

10th Mountain Hut & Trail System

10th Mountain Trail is located in the White River
and San Isabel National Forests
under agreement with the Forest Service, USDA.

Scale 1:24,000

SCALE IN MILES

Hut ■

Trailhead ●

MN 12°

Trails are marked by blue diamonds, except in
wilderness areas where trails are marked by tree blazes.

This map is not a substitute for good route finding skills,
it is just an aid to help locate routes.
These are suggested routes only.
Trails are not groomed and their exact location may vary.

© 1989 - 10th Mountain Trail Association

Teacup
Bowl

TWO ELK
Pass

To Vail

8.2

WHITE RIVER
NATIONAL FOREST

Battle

Turkey Creek

8.3
8.5
9.8

2.53 miles to **Red Cliff**
6.45 miles to **Fowler/Hilliard Hut**
6.80 miles to **Shrine Mountain Inn**

8.3
9.4
9.5

3.30 miles to **Red Cliff**
5.68 miles to **Fowler/Hilliard Hut**

Gaging
Sta

Gaging Sta

8.5
9.5
9.8

Turkey Creek

Tates
Gulch

Wearyman Creek

**Red Cliff
Trailhead**
Mine 9,690'

9.4

2.25 miles to **Fowler/Hi**
4.54 miles to **Shrine Mou**

Red Cliff
(Redcliff PO)
Gaging
Sta

Iron
Mtn

BM
8763
2668

PIPELINE

Hornsilver
Mountain

JEEP

Resolution Narrows

0.30 m
6.49 m

Homestake
Campground

**Fowler/Hilliar
Hut**
Resolution
Mountain
11,500'

9.11

Hornsilver
Campground

0.50 miles to **Fowler Hilliard Hut**
4.51 miles to **Pando**
5.94 miles to **Camp Hale**
7.31 miles to **Schuss/Zesiger Hut**
8.48 miles to **Red Cliff**

1.10 miles to **Fowler/Hilliard Hut**
3.91 miles to **Pando**
5.34 miles to **Camp Hale**
6.71 miles to **Schuss/Zesiger Hut**

9.1

To Pando

To Camp Hale

9.2
9.10

Resolution Road

continue

110

ARAPAHO
NATIONAL FOREST

EAGLES NEST WILDERNESS

1.88 miles to **Shrine Mountain Inn**
7.45 miles to **Red Cliff**
14.8 miles to **Vail**

0.38 miles to **Shrine Mountain Inn**
2.35 miles to **Vail Pass**
8.95 miles to **Red Cliff**
16.3 miles to **Vail**

Shrine Pass
BM 11,089

Black Lake Glades

8.6

Shrine Mountain Inn
11,209'

Shrine Mountain

8.1

BM 10549
Vail Pass

8.4
9.7

Vail Pass Trailhead
10,580'

miles to **Shrine Mountain Inn**
miles to **Fowler/Hilliard Hut**

West Tennite Creek

9.6

Wilder Gulch

To Fowler/Hilliard Hut
Shrine Mountain Inn

Smith Gulch

To Copper Mountain

RED CLIFF VAIL PASS
U.S.G.S. QUADS
PANDO COPPER MOUNTAIN

Ptarmigan Hill

9.3
9.6

Ptarmigan Pass

Ptarmigan Pass

9.3

Uneva Peak

Uneva Pass

111

conifer forest at a red stock gate. Follow an obvious road cut through the forest 1/4 mile S to the Shrine Mountain Inn. Use your map, compass, and altimeter for insurance. The large inn is visible from several hundred feet down the road.

REVERSE ROUTE DESCRIPTION: From the Shrine Mountain Inn ski the 10th Mountain marked trail downhill N through clearings, then NE to Shrine Pass. Pick up the Shrine Pass road here and follow it SE 2 1/3 miles to the Vail Pass Trailhead.

SAFETY NOTES: This is certainly the easiest trailhead to hut trip on the 10th Mountain suggested routes. As a result, it is used by many novice ski tourers — as it should be. But every skier should remember that given poor visibility during a storm, even this simple trail could be dangerous.

SUMMER: The Shrine Pass Road is a good cycling route. Hikers can explore Shrine Mountain and the surrounding drainages. Horse people can ride the road, but there is lots of car traffic.

8.2

Shrine Mountain Inn — Vail Trailhead via Commando Run

DIFFICULTY: Expert
TIME: 13 hours up, 8 hours down
DISTANCE: 16 1/4 miles
ELEVATION GAIN: (Inn to Vail) 2,080 feet; elevation loss: 5,069 feet
10TH MTN MAP: Resolution Mountain
USGS MAPS: Vail Pass, Red Cliff, Vail East

This is a popular, traditional tour. It is named after the men of the 10th Mountain Division who used the route for informal training during the Camp Hale days in the 1940's (see Appendix 2). For the first 8 miles the Commando Run follows a superb timbered ridge with several summits that poke up just above timber line, offering great views. This route is higher and longer than most 10th Mountain suggested routes and has more downhill skiing. Thus, you'll find it a nice alternative if you have the skills to enjoy it. The Commando Run is a section of the Colorado Trail, a "transstate" route that connects Durango and Denver. The Colorado Trail is marked with small white triangles that say Colorado Trail.

The traditional Commando Run starts at Vail Pass. To conform to the 10th Mountain suggested routes however, this description starts at the Shrine Mountain Inn.

ROUTE DESCRIPTION: From the Shrine Mountain Inn, ski back down the 10th Mountain suggested route (reverse route 8.1) to Shrine Pass. Ski the snow-covered Shrine Pass Road 1 1/4 miles down Turkey Creek (good downhill cruising) to 10,660 feet. Leave the Shrine Pass Road here (time for skins) and take a right (N) turn onto the Lime Creek Road. There is a sign here that says Lime Creek Road No. 728, but the sign may be covered by snow.

Ski up the Lime Creek Road 1/2 mile to a low-angled area (10,990 feet). The road forks here, with a sign indicating Timber Creek to the right and Lime Creek to the left. Take a left (W) and ski several hundred feet up the Lime Creek Road to a lightly timbered area. This is where the real back-country skiing begins.

Watch carefully for an indistinct signpost on the right that says Colorado Trail. Turn right (N) off the Lime Creek Road and follow the Colorado Trail to the upper left (W) of the light timber, then contour around the left (W) side of point 11,611 at about the 11,400-foot level. From the W side of point 11,611 follow the ridge to the summits of points 11,710 and 11,696. Enjoy the terrific views (strip your skins), then descend N to a heavily timbered saddle. Stay on the ridge from the saddle, climb a bit, then contour around the left (W) side of point 11,618. Take care with your route finding here, as you can get too far west and end up in Two Elk Creek. Descend the ridge to Two Elk Pass and enjoy the good open views. Dig out your map, spot the back bowls of Vail Ski Area (all the south-facing terrain W of Siberia Peak is part of the ski area), and identify your next goal — point 11,816 to the NW. This is Siberia Peak, the highest point on the Commando Run. Put on your skins and sweat it out.

At the summit of Siberia Peak you have two choices. For the classic ridge run, continue W from the summit of Siberia Peak along a narrow ridge crest, gradually deviate to the S until you are following the ski boundary, which eventually takes you to a catwalk on the ridge. Follow the catwalk to the restaurant/lift terminus known as Far East, pick up a trail map, then ski N down the ski area to Vail. Take care not to ski down into the Vail bowls, as you need a lift ticket to get back up!

For a more woodsy escapade, drop N from the summit of Siberia Peak, then take the fall line, staying a bit E of center (skier's right). This area is called Mushroom Bowl and, if the snow is good, it will give some "fine turning". As you near the apex of Mushroom Bowl be sure you are on the north side of the drainage, then intersect the snow-covered Mill Creek Road. Follow the road down Mill Creek, where you'll enter the Vail Ski Area. Pick up a trail map and plan a route down to Vail Village (see Chapter 1, Vail Trailhead for the Commando Run).

REVERSE ROUTE DESCRIPTION: Skiing the Commando Run from Vail is an arduous trek that will take all but the strongest groups more than one day (without ski lifts). From the Vail Trailhead for the Commando Run, ski or ride to the lift 10 terminus. Head E and into Mill Creek, then follow the snow-covered Mill Creek Road as it climbs the valley on the north side of Mill Creek.

At 10,400 feet the road begins to wander up long switchbacks. Leave the road and climb a fairly direct line to the summit of Siberia Peak. Drop to Two Elk Pass (if the skiing is good strip your skins, then re-skin at the pass) and stay on the ridge S of Two Elk Pass for 1 ¾ miles to points 11,695 and 11,710. Take care in the timber past Two Elk Pass, it is all too easy to drop into Two Elk Creek.

Still sticking to the ridge, swing E at point 11,710 and ridge run to point 11,611. Drop down the southeast side of point 11,611 to intersect the Lime Creek Road in a sparsely timbered area at 10,840 feet. Ski the Lime Creek Road downhill E to a low-angled area and continue downhill E to the Shrine Pass Road. Climb the Shrine Pass Road to Shrine Pass, then follow route 8.1 to the Shrine Mountain Inn or Vail Pass.

You can also get to Siberia Peak by riding Vail ski lifts 21 and 22. If you use ski lifts to access the backcountry, be sure to exit the ski area at the designated gates. You can get weather and avalanche information by dialing 4652 on the red phones within the Vail Ski Area.

SAFETY NOTES: The east side of Siberia Peak is steep and often capped by a dangerous cornice. Other slopes on the peak are usually wind scoured into stability, but should be carefully examined for avalanche hazard. Good emergency egress can be made down Two Elk Creek to the bottom of the Vail back bowl ski lifts. Remember that the lifts may be closed, and that Two Elk Creek has some narrow sections with possible bank-sluffs and hazard from avalanche control in the Vail bowls.

SUMMER: Hikers, equestrians, and mountain cyclists will find that, with the amount of use this trail is getting, the Commando Run section of the Colorado Trail is well maintained, easy to follow, and fun. Cyclists must occasionally shoulder their steeds.

8.3

Red Cliff Trailhead — Shrine Mountain Inn via Shrine Pass Road

DIFFICULTY: Light Intermediate
TIME: 7 hours up
DISTANCE: 9 miles
ELEVATION GAIN: 2,529 feet
10TH MTN MAP: Resolution Mountain
USGS MAPS: Red Cliff, Vail Pass

This 10th Mountain suggested route follows the well-used, snow-covered Shrine Pass Road. It is a long trip with comparatively easy navigation. Thus, this is a good "classroom tour" for the freshman backcountry skier.

ROUTE DESCRIPTION: In the town of Red Cliff find the Shrine Pass Road and reconnoiter your parking (see Chapter 1, Red Cliff Trailhead). In general, remember that you will follow the distinct, snow-covered Shrine Pass Road up the Turkey Creek drainage to Shrine Pass. At Shrine Pass you leave the main road and take a dedicated 10th Mountain suggested route to the Shrine Mountain Inn.

Start with waxed skis. At 2 ½ miles (9,000 feet) on the Shrine Pass Road you'll pass an obvious intersection at Wearyman Creek. Here route 9.3 takes off to the right (S). Take care to stay on the Shrine Pass Road and ski 4 miles up Turkey Creek to the only switchback on the road in a large clearing at 10,360 feet. In poor weather there is the possibility of losing the road here, especially with high winds. Just remember that the road leaves the gut of the drainage and climbs E through the clearing (staying on the north side of the drainage). The important thing is to find the road as it re-enters timber at the east end of the clearing, otherwise you'll have to beat some dense timber and brush.

Just ¼ mile into the timber (10,660 feet) you'll pass the left (N) turn-off of the Lime Creek Road (see route 8.2). Stay on the Shrine Pass Road and continue E then SE through light timber to Shrine Pass, a nondescript, flat clearing that forms the divide between Turkey Creek and West Tenmile Creek. Ski to the east end of the Shrine Pass clearing. Look for a White River National Forest sign facing E. Ski W from this sign several hundred yards across a clear area and enter a conifer forest at a red stock gate. Follow an obvious road cut through the forest ¼ mile S to the Shrine Mountain Inn. Use your map, compass, and altimeter for insurance. The large inn is visible from several hundred feet down the road.

REVERSE ROUTE DESCRIPTION: Take care to identify Shrine Pass, then ski the snow-covered Shrine Pass Road to Red Cliff.

SAFETY NOTES: Be sure to stay on the Shrine Pass Road, as there are several tempting turn-offs along the way. Don't let the ease of following this road lull you into complacent route finding—use your skills. The Shrine Pass Road is heavily used by snowmobiles, so keep your eyes and ears open, and be courteous.

SUMMER: This is a fine horse, hike, or bike route. The Shrine Pass Road has heavy auto use in the summer.

8.4

Shrine Mountain Inn to Fowler/Hilliard Hut via Shrine Mountain Ridge

DIFFICULTY: Intermediate (Expert in poor weather)
TIME: 6 hours
DISTANCE: 6 ¾ miles
ELEVATION GAIN: 1,221 feet; elevation loss: 930 feet
10TH MTN MAP: Resolution Mountain
USGS MAPS: Vail Pass, Red Cliff, Pando

This 10th Mountain suggested route begins with a terrific ridge run and some good downhill skiing, but ends with a long "treadmill" logging road through the forest. Before you start, be certain that the weather will be good enough for travel above timber line (see Appendix 4). Several groups have reported near disasters from trying the Shrine Mountain Ridge during wind storms. If you're looking for branch routes from the Shrine Mountain Inn, use this route to climb Shrine Mountain. Experts will find some skiing on the east face of Shrine Mountain, but intermediates should retrace their steps back to the Inn.

ROUTE DESCRIPTION: From the Shrine Mountain Inn climb SW 1 mile and 531 vertical feet to Shrine Mountain Saddle (11,740 feet). This is the first saddle SE of Shrine Mountain. Enjoy the awesome view of the Holy Cross Mountains and take the time to evaluate your position. For the next 1 ¼ miles the trail stays above timber line, skirting and gradually dropping around the west side of Shrine Mountain Ridge. In poor or deteriorating weather you should consider turning back (see Chapter 9 for other routes to the Fowler/Hilliard Hut).

Continuing from Shrine Mountain Saddle, use your compass, map, and altimeter to make an accurate dropping traverse to timber line on the southwest face of the ridge, on the north side of the Wearyman Creek drainage. From here you can ski directly down to the apex of the drainage at 11,000 feet, or take a more gradual dropping traverse SE into the drainage. With good snow you can make some fine turns with the former option. Novice downhillers should stick to the latter.

At 11,000 feet in the Wearyman Creek drainage you'll be in an elongated park. Near the lower (W) end of the park find the channel where Wearyman Creek leaves the park. Here you'll find the marked 10th Mountain suggested route. It crosses to the west side of Wearyman Creek for a short distance, enters the trees on a snowcat trail, and drops down a steep hill to a small clearing. From the clearing stay on the 10th Mountain suggested route as it climbs SW through forest for a short distance to a distinct logging road (10,880 feet). Follow this road SW; it is very low-angled and seems to go on forever. Persevere, perhaps using cross country wax, and ski 1 ¾ miles on the road to the 11,200-foot level, where it begins to climb SE via a series of low-angled, inefficient switchbacks. If you're using wax, you might like these switchbacks. Many skiers, however, put their skins on and cut directly up the hill, using the switchbacks for reference, and regaining the 10th Mountain suggested route at the last switchback.

Whatever your choice in routes, once you gain the ridge at the 11,400-foot level (Ptarmigan Ridge), follow it W then SW ⅓ mile to the Fowler/Hilliard Hut. You cannot see the hut until you reach the small knob several hundred yards SE of the site.

There is a good variation for this route, that gives you a lot more high altitude ridge-running. Simply stay on Shrine Mountain Ridge all the way to the saddle that divides the Wearyman and Wilder drainages. From the saddle, climb S to Ptarmigan Pass, then ascend the ridge W to the summit of Ptarmigan Hill. Drop down the west side of Ptarmigan Hill to a distinct road cut. Ski the road W as it skirts the south side of Ptarmigan Ridge and then intersects the 10th Mountain marked route 8.4 leading W along the ridge to the Fowler/Hilliard Hut.

SAFETY NOTES: Take care with route finding and weather on the alpine portion of this route. There is an active avalanche path on the south face of Ptarmigan Hill.

SUMMER: This route is a fine hike. A short section of trail, connecting Wearyman Creek with the logging road to the SW, is only a marked route through the forest with no real path. Cyclists will enjoy all the roads in the area. Shrine Mountain Ridge is too high and rough for equestrian traffic, but the roads and "real" trails in the area are fine horse routes.

8.5

Shrine Mountain Inn to Fowler/Hilliard Hut via Shrine Pass Road and Wearyman Creek Road

DIFFICULTY: Expert
TIME: 15 hours
DISTANCE: 14 miles
ELEVATION GAIN: 2,670 feet; elevation loss: 2,379 feet
10TH MTN MAP: Resolution Mountain
USGS MAPS: Vail Pass, Red Cliff, Pando

This is the only low-altitude route connecting the Shrine Mountain Inn to the Fowler/Hilliard Hut. It is rated expert because of it's length.

ROUTE DESCRIPTION: To begin, ski the 10th Mountain marked trail from the Shrine Mountain Inn N then NE down to Shrine Pass, a nondescript, lightly timbered flat that forms the divide between Turkey Creek and West Tenmile Creek. Turn NW at the pass onto the Shrine Pass Road. This road will be indistinct at the pass, but easier to identify as you ski lower into the Turkey Creek drainage. Ski down the Shrine Pass Road 6 miles to 9,000 feet. Turn left (S) off the Shrine Pass Road onto the Wearyman Creek Road; this intersection is obvious. Follow route 9.5 7 ¾ miles to the Fowler/Hilliard Hut.

SAFETY NOTES: This is a very long route. If you reach the low point of the route (on Shrine Pass Road) very late, consider bailing out in Red Cliff.

SUMMER: All these roads make fine bicycle routes.

Atop Shrine Pass headed west. This pass is a nondescript clearing.

8.6

Black Lake Glades from Shrine Mountain Inn

DIFFICULTY: Intermediate
TIME: Half or full day depending on the amount of skiing
DISTANCE: 4 ¾ miles round trip
ELEVATION GAIN: 776 feet round trip
10TH MTN MAP: Resolution Mountain
USGS MAP: Vail Pass

Within a day of the Shrine Mountain Inn, the best place to do some downhill skiing is the Black Lake Glades. You can reach this area from the Inn or from Vail Pass. One run nets you about 700 vertical feet of skiing and you can push as many laps as your lungs allow.

ROUTE DESCRIPTION: The Black Lake Glades are easy to find. At Vail Pass just look NW and you'll see the gladed north-facing slopes dropping to the Black Lakes. To ascend, skin up through the glades or use the Shrine Pass Road (see route 8.1) as a route to saddle 11,156, and explore downhill from there. If you're skiing from the Shrine Mountain Inn, head back down to Shrine Pass (see route 8.1). Experts can head N from the pass to point 11,325, then ski to Black Lake No. 2; intermediates should follow the Shrine Pass Road SE to the aforementioned saddle 11,156 and ski from there. In general, you'll find more mellow terrain the closer you are to the Vail Pass Trailhead.

SAFETY NOTES: Though the Black Lake Glades are not classic slide paths, there can be pocket slab avalanches on the steeper slopes. If you're staying at the Inn, give yourself enough time to return before dark.

SUMMER: This is trailless ski terrain unsuitable for bikes and horses. The sparsely timbered areas around Shrine Pass are good for alpine hikes.

Chapter 9 • Fowler/Hilliard Hut

Owned by 10th Mountain, the Fowler/Hilliard Hut sits at timber line about ½ mile northeast of the summit of Resolution Mountain. The south windows give you a marvelous view towards the Schuss/Zesiger Hut and some of the highest peaks in Colorado.

ELEVATION: 11,500 feet
COUNTY: Eagle
TEXT MAP: pp. 110-111, 138-139
10TH MTN MAP: Res. Mt., Chicago Rdg.
USGS MAP: Pando
TRAILHEADS: Pando, Red Cliff, Vail Pass

Up to 16 people can find bed space in the Fowler/Hilliard Hut. It has photo-electric lighting and a roomy kitchen replete with utensils and two gas cooktops. The sleeping area is all upstairs, with communal eating and lounging downstairs. This averts "party angst" for those bedding early. Loud noise still penetrates, however, so remember your earplugs.

The Fowler/Hilliard Hut was built in 1989 with funds from over 260 people and businesses. It is a a memorial to well-known Denver residents Ann Fowler and Ed Hilliard who were killed in a climbing accident on North Maroon Peak, south of Aspen.

More than 6 fine ski routes connect the Fowler/Hilliard Hut to other huts and trailheads. Intermediate level skiers will enjoy the Resolution Creek route (9.2), or they can take a slightly more direct climb on the McAllister Gulch route (9.1). The Wearyman Creek route (9.5) is long, but avoids travel above timber line. Experts can enjoy a high route over Hornsilver Mountain (route 9.4) and a less direct alternate high route that climbs over Ptarmigan Hill (route 9.3).

For a northerly ski-through, you'll want to use the Shrine Mountain Ridge route (9.7) to go north to the Shrine Mountain Inn. For a ski south to the Schuss/Zesiger Hut, take the High Route (9.9) or Pearl Creek (route 9.10). If the weather looks scary, consider low routes 9.8 and 9.10 for ski-throughs.

If you love "base skiing", you can't do much better than the Fowler/Hilliard Hut. From the southeast bowl of Resolution Mountain, to the low-angled glades north of the hut, to Ptarmigan Hill — there are turns for everyone. Many groups spend one night at the Fowler/Hilliard, get a ski run the next morning, then ski on to a trailhead or another hut. You can get in a few turns this way, especially if you take a more direct line down to your chosen route. But you should consider staying for at least 2 nights at the Fowler/Hilliard and enjoy a day of "light pack cruising" around the hut.

9.1

Pando Trailhead — Fowler/Hilliard Hut via McAllister Gulch

DIFFICULTY: Intermediate
TIME: 5 hours down, 3 ½ hours up
DISTANCE: 5 ¼ miles
ELEVATION GAIN: 2,500 feet; elevation loss: 200 feet
10TH MTN MAP: Chicago Ridge
USGS MAP: Pando

This is the most direct 10th Mountain suggested route to the Fowler/Hilliard Hut. Since you pass over a high saddle, keep an eye on the weather.

ROUTE DESCRIPTION: Begin at the Pando Trailhead. Ski E across a bridge over the Eagle River, then ¼ mile E and NE across Camp Hale. You'll intersect a snow-covered north/south road at the base of the mountain. Turn left (N) and ski ½ mile to a right turn (NE) onto the McAllister Gulch jeep road. This is where you leave the valley (put your skins on). Follow the road as it makes a climbing traverse N, then swings NE into McAllister Gulch. At about 9,400 feet, you'll encounter some private property signs. These designate property on the northwest side of the road — skiers should stay on the road.

Put your head down and work the long 2-mile climb to the head of McAllister Gulch. At 10,440 feet take a right turn SE and continue slugging it out to 11,300 feet on the southwest ridge of Resolution Mountain (intersection with route 9.2).

Climb the ridge crest for a short distance to 11,400 feet. Next, take a ¾-mile climbing traverse NE then N across the west face of Resolution Mountain, ending at the 11,700-foot saddle (Resolution Saddle) on the northwest ridge. On a clear day you can see the hut from here — a welcome sight. Ski down E from the saddle and cut a short traverse that leads you to a distinct east/west cleft called the Resolution Narrows. Take care to not ski N downhill from the saddle. Continue E down the cleft to the Fowler/Hilliard Hut in a clearing at 11,500 feet. To get some "bonus turns", experts should consider ascending Resolution Mountain from the southwest ridge, then cutting turns down to the hut.

REVERSE ROUTE DESCRIPTION:

To ski from the hut, take the time for some map reading on the dining room table. Identify the distinct east/west cleft of the Resolution Narrows that climbs up the north side of Resolution Mountain. Ski the Resolution Narrows to the 11,700-foot Resolution Saddle. Take a left (S) here and glide across the west face of Resolution Mountain to 11,400 feet on the southwest ridge. Drop down the southwest ridge 100 vertical feet, then turn right (NW), drop into McAllister Gulch, and follow the McAllister Gulch jeep trail to the Eagle River valley and Camp Hale. Ski ½ mile south in Camp Hale, then turn W, ski across the flats, and cross a bridge over the Eagle River to the Pando Trailhead at Highway 24.

If visibility is poor in Camp Hale you may have trouble finding the exact trailhead and bridge. In this case, you can strike cross country to Highway 24, your only obstacles being the Eagle River and up to a mile of trail to break out. In midwinter there are usually snow bridges over the Eagle River.

SAFETY NOTES: There can be slide danger on the open slopes of Resolution Mountain. Be aware of cornices on all the ridges. The trails out of Camp Hale are quite often used by snowmobiles, so keep your ears open.

SUMMER: The McAllister Gulch jeep road is a fine hike, bike, and horse route. It connects to the Hornsilver Mountain jeep trail (see route 9.4), but does not connect to the Fowler/Hilliard Hut. To get to the hut with a bike you can portage from the 11,700-foot saddle down Resolution Narrows.

9.2
Pando Trailhead — Fowler/Hilliard Hut via Resolution Creek

DIFFICULTY: Intermediate
TIME: 5 ½ hours up, 4 hours down
DISTANCE: 6 ½ miles
ELEVATION GAIN: 2,500 feet; elevation loss: 200 feet
10TH MTN MAP: Chicago Ridge
USGS MAP: Pando

This longer trailhead to hut route has easier downhill skiing than route 9.1. The two routes join together for the climb around Resolution Mountain. You'd have to toss a coin to decide between the Pando or Camp Hale trailheads for "best trailhead" for this route. Base your choice on parking and bridges; the route here is described from the Pando Trailhead. This is a 10th Mountain suggested route.

ROUTE DESCRIPTION: From the Pando Trailhead ski E across the main north/south Camp Hale Road, across a bridge over the Eagle River, then E and NE to intersect a snow-covered road running N/S at the base of the mountain. You can ski this road S and intersect the Resolution Road, but to avoid "sled" traffic the following is a better route. Ski the road at the base of the mountain N a short distance, then turn right and ski SE up through a gulch E of point 9,540 (again, this is not the main Camp Hale Road). One mile from Pando you intersect the distinct Resolution Road. Take a left (NE) and ski 2 ½ miles up the Resolution Road to 9,960 feet.

Leave the Resolution Road here and take a left (NW) onto a marked 10th Mountain trail. The blue diamonds take you up to a 10,940-foot saddle on the southwest ridge of Resolution Mountain. Most of this trail follows a distinct trail cut through forest. In the occasional clearing, take the time to really zero in on the route with your map. Remember: diamonds are for dummies.

Climb the southwest ridge of Resolution Mountain ¾ mile to 11,400 feet (you'll pass the intersection of route 9.1 at 11,300 feet). Next, take a ¾-mile climbing traverse NE then N across the west face of Resolution Mountain, ending at 11,700-foot Resolution Saddle on the northwest ridge of Resolution Mountain. Ski down E from the saddle and cut a short traverse that leads you to a distinct east/west cleft called the Resolution Narrows. Take care to not ski N downhill from the saddle. Continue E down the cleft to the Fowler/Hilliard Hut in a clearing at 11,500 feet. In clear weather, the hut is visible from Resolution Saddle. To get some "bonus turns", experts should consider ascending Resolution Mountain, then cutting turns down to the hut.

REVERSE ROUTE DESCRIPTION: To ski from the hut, take the time for some map reading on the dining room table. Put on your skins. Identify the distinct east/west cleft (Resolution Narrows) that climbs up the north side of Resolution Mountain and ski the cleft to the 11,700-foot saddle. Remove your skins. Take a left (S) here and glide across the west face of Resolution Mountain to 11,400 feet on the southwest ridge. Drop down the southwest ridge (at 11,300 feet you'll pass the right turn onto route 9.1) to a saddle at 10,950 feet. Turn left (SE) and drop down switchbacks 980 vertical feet to the distinct Resolution Road. Ski the Resolution Road SW 2 miles to Camp Hale. For the Pando Trailhead, take a right just before you make a final short drop into the flats of Camp Hale and ski N on a road tucked in behind point 9,540. Just N of point 9,540 you'll intersect a main north/south snow-covered road. Take a left (S) here, turn W, and ski across the flats to a bridge over the Eagle River. The Pando Trailhead is several hundred feet W of the bridge.

If visibility is poor in Camp Hale, you may have trouble finding the Pando

Trailhead and bridge. In this case, you can strike cross country to Highway 24, your only obstacles being the Eagle River and up to a mile of trail to break out. In midwinter, there are usually snow bridges over the Eagle River.

SAFETY NOTES: There can be slide danger on the open slopes of Resolution Mountain. Be aware of cornices on all the ridges. The trails out of Camp Hale are used by snowmobiles quite often.

SUMMER: This route is fine for hiking. The section of trail from Resolution Creek climbing to Resolution Mountain is a marked ski route with no footpath for horse or bike travel. The Resolution Road is a good bicycle route.

9.3
Pando Trailhead — Fowler/Hilliard Hut via Ptarmigan Hill Traverse

DIFFICULTY: Advanced
TIME: 8 hours up, 6 hours down
DISTANCE: 9 miles
ELEVATION GAIN: 2,983 feet; elevation loss: 683 feet
10TH MTN MAP: Chicago Ridge
USGS MAP: Pando

This alternate route is long, but quite rewarding. It includes a grand 2-mile alpine traverse with a 12,143-foot summit.

ROUTE DESCRIPTION: From the Pando Trailhead follow route 9.2 to 9,960 feet on the Resolution Road, where route 9.2 climbs NW. Instead, stay on the distinct Resolution Road for 3 miles to Ptarmigan Pass, a broad saddle at 11,765 feet. Leave the road here and ascend the east ridge of Ptarmigan Hill. At the summit of Ptarmigan Hill, you'll find a good view and some wooden shacks that cover antennae. Descend the west face of Ptarmigan Hill to a distinct saddle at 11,580 feet. This can be a fun little ski run, but may have some difficult snow. Remember, "there is no such thing as bad snow — just poor skiers".

From the saddle, follow a road cut that contours through sparse timber around the south side of point 11,683, then leads to the 11,480-foot saddle where you converge with route 9.5/8.4. Continue 1/3 mile W and SW along the ridge to the Fowler/Hilliard Hut. The hut is not visible until you top a small, 40-foot high mound several hundred feet E of the hut.

There is one very worthy variation to this trail; it's called the Ptarmigan

Shoulder route. Instead of skiing all the way to Ptarmigan Pass, turn off the Resolution Road at 10,704 feet and ski N up the east side of an intermittent stream in a gulch. At 11,000 feet take a climbing traverse W to the ridge leading up to point 11,683. Ascend the ridge to the road that contours the southwest side of 11,683. This road is the last leg of the Ptarmigan Hill Traverse described above. The Ptarmigan Shoulder also makes a fine descent route.

REVERSE ROUTE DESCRIPTION: The Ptarmigan Hill Traverse is a nice way to ski from the Fowler/Hilliard Hut back to the Pando Trailhead (or see Wilder Gulch in route 9.6). From the hut follow the 10th Mountain suggested route ⅓ mile E and NE to the 11,480-foot saddle. Leave the 10th Mountain suggested route and continue on a distinct road cut that traverses the southwest face of point 11,683, leading to the 11,580-foot saddle below the west face of Ptarmigan Hill. Ascend the west face to the summit of Ptarmigan Hill, then descend the east ridge to Ptarmigan Pass. From Ptarmigan Pass, ski the Resolution Road 6 ½ miles down Resolution Creek to Camp Hale.

For the Pando Trailhead, take a right just before you make a final short drop into the flats of Camp Hale, and ski N on a road tucked in behind point 9,540. Just N of point 9,540 you'll intersect a main north/south snow-covered road. Take a left (S) here, turn W, and ski across the flats to a bridge over the Eagle River. The Pando Trailhead is several hundred feet W of the bridge.

If visibility is poor in Camp Hale you may have trouble finding the Pando Trailhead and bridge. In this case you can strike cross country to Highway 24, your only obstacles being the Eagle River and up to a mile of trail to break out. In midwinter there are usually snow bridges over the Eagle River.

SAFETY NOTES: The road that traverses around the south ridge of Ptarmigan Hill (as shown on the USGS map) is tempting, but it crosses several slide paths on the south face of Ptarmigan Hill. Indeed, these paths sometimes run over the road lower down. Use proper precautions. Beware of cornices on the Ptarmigan Hill summit. Get an early start for this route.

SUMMER: This is a good hike or horse ride. Superfit cyclists might enjoy it as well, but the climb to Ptarmigan Hill from Ptarmigan Pass would be a portage.

9.4

Red Cliff Trailhead — Fowler/Hilliard Hut via Hornsilver Mountain

DIFFICULTY: Intermediate
TIME: 10 hours up, 7 hours down
DISTANCE: 9 miles
ELEVATION GAIN: 3,180 feet; elevation loss: 360 feet
10TH MTN MAP: Resolution Mountain
USGS MAPS: Pando, Red Cliff

This 10th Mountain suggested route includes a scenic alpine ridge run. It is long and arduous, but rewarding.

ROUTE DESCRIPTION: Begin at the Red Cliff Trailhead. Ski up the distinct snow-covered Shrine Pass Road 2 1/2 miles to 9,000 feet. You can wax to here, but put on your skins for the climb ahead. Leave the Shrine Pass Road and turn right (S) on the well-marked and heavily traveled Wearyman Creek Road. Ski up the Wearyman Creek Road 3/4 mile to 9,280 feet. Leave the Wearyman Creek drainage here and take a hard right on a westerly climbing traverse on the Hornsilver Mountain jeep trail. This turn is fairly obvious, but take care with your map reading.

Now the real push begins. Stay on the marked 10th Mountain suggested route as it winds through timber, climbing 2 ½ miles SW, to where you intersect the west ridge of Hornsilver Mountain at 11,200 feet near timber line. From here climb the ridge E to the summit of Hornsilver Mountain, then stick to the crest of Hornsilver Ridge as you ski 1 mile SE over one small bump to a major saddle at 11,450 feet. Stay on the ridge and continue climbing SE towards the summit of Resolution Mountain. After ½ mile and 242 feet of climbing, you'll reach another, smaller saddle at 11,700 feet (Resolution Saddle), a short distance below the summit of Resolution Mountain.

Leave the ridge here by skiing from the north side of the saddle on a short traverse E that leads you to a distinct east/west cleft (the Resolution Narrows) that leads downhill E to the hut. Take care to not ski N downhill from the saddle – if you do this, you'll miss the cleft and have to camp in Wearyman Creek. Ski E down the cleft to the Fowler/Hilliard Hut in a clearing at 11,500 feet. The hut is visible from Resolution Saddle and from the east slopes of Resolution Mountain. To get some "bonus turns", experts should consider ascending Resolution Mountain from the southwest ridge, then cutting turns down to the hut.

REVERSE ROUTE DESCRIPTION: To ski this route from the hut, use your map to identify the distinct east/west cleft (Resolution Narrows) that climbs up the north side of Resolution Mountain. Ski the cleft to the 11,700-foot Resolution Saddle on the northwest ridge of Resolution Mountain. From the saddle, descend the ridge to another, better defined saddle at 11,458 feet. Stay on the ridge and ski to the summit of Hornsilver Mountain. Drop down the west ridge of Hornsilver Mountain to 11,200 feet, then turn N and descend through forest into the Wearyman Creek drainage.

At Wearyman Creek you intersect the distinct, well-used Wearyman Creek jeep road. Ski this road downvalley ¾ mile to the snow-covered Shrine Pass Road, which you than ski downvalley 2 ½ miles to the Red Cliff Trailhead.

SAFETY NOTES: Take care with cornices on the Hornsilver and Resolution ridges. This is a long route with several miles of skiing near or above timber line. Thus, get an early start and be prepared for wind chill.

SUMMER: This route is a good hike or horse ride. Most cyclists will find good riding on the roads in the Wearyman Creek drainage. If you are a fit, expert cyclist, explore the Hornsilver Mountain section of the route.

9.5

Red Cliff Trailhead — Fowler/Hilliard Hut via Wearyman Creek Road

DIFFICULTY: Intermediate
TIME: 12 hours up, 9 hours down
DISTANCE: 10 miles
ELEVATION GAIN: 3,000 feet; elevation loss: 180 feet
10TH MTN MAP: Resolution Mountain
USGS MAPS: Red Cliff, Pando

As a route to or from the Red Cliff Trailhead, this alternate route lacks the spectacular ridge run of route 9.4, but it could be a better choice in terrible weather. Since it's not a 10th Mountain suggested route, the Wearyman Creek Road section is not marked with the ubiquitous blue diamonds. However, it is often packed by snowmobile and follows distinct logging roads cut through the forest.

ROUTE DESCRIPTION: Starting at the Red Cliff Trailhead ski up the Shrine Pass Road 2 ½ miles to 9,000 feet. Here take the obvious right turn of the Wearyman Creek Road into the Wearyman Creek drainage. To be doubly sure about this spot, just count the drainages on your right as you ski from Red Cliff, then correlate these with your map.

Follow the Wearyman Creek Road ¾ mile up the Wearyman Creek drainage to 9,280 feet. Here, route 9.4 leaves the road and heads W up the side of the drainage. (If the weather has improved, consider route 9.4.)

To stick with the 9.5 alternate route, just continue up the Wearyman Creek Road. Though unmarked by 10th Mountain, it is distinct and heavily used. After a long 4-mile pull you'll arrive at an elongated park (11,000 feet). ⅛ mile up from the lower (W) end of the park find the channel where Wearyman Creek leaves the park. Here you'll find the marked 10th Mountain suggested route. It follows the west side of Wearyman Creek for a short distance and crosses to the southeast side of the creek. Here you leave the creek and drop down a steep hill (a strong snowplow is useful) about 150 vertical feet to a small clearing. From the clearing stay on the 10th Mountain suggested route as it climbs SW through forest for a short distance to a distinct logging road.

Climb this road SW; it is very low-angled and seems to go on forever. Persevere, perhaps using cross country wax, and ski 1 ¾ miles on the road to the 11,200-foot level, where it begins to climb SE via a series of low-angled, inefficient switchbacks. If you're using wax, you might like these switchbacks. Many skiers, however, put their skins on and cut directly up the hill, using the switchbacks for reference, and regaining the 10th Mountain suggested route at the last switchback.

Whatever your choice in routes, once you gain the ridge (Ptarmigan Ridge) at the 11,400-foot level, follow it W then SW ⅓ mile through sparse timber to the Fowler/Hilliard Hut. You cannot see the hut until you reach the top of a small 40-foot high mound several hundred feet E of the site.

REVERSE ROUTE DESCRIPTION: This route is simple to reverse. Follow route 9.7 to the elongated park at 11,000 feet in the Wearyman Creek drainage. Ski to the west end of the park and find the distinct cut of the Wearyman Creek Road. Follow the Wearyman Creek Road 4 miles to the snow-covered Shrine Pass Road. Take a left (W) on the Shrine Pass Road and ski the road 2 ½ miles to the Red Cliff Trailhead.

SAFETY NOTES: This route is long, so get an early start. Beware of bank sluffs and larger slides on the mountainside above the Wearyman Creek Road. Also, be aware that helicopter skiers occasionally use these slopes, and they could trigger slides.

SUMMER: Horses and hikers will enjoy this whole route. Cyclists will have to portage the section between the elongated park and the road to the SW.

9.6

Vail Pass Trailhead — Fowler/Hilliard Hut via Wilder Gulch and Ptarmigan Hill

DIFFICULTY: Advanced
TIME: 7 hours up, 4 ½ hours down
DISTANCE: 7 miles
ELEVATION GAIN: 1,573 feet; elevation loss: 683 feet
10TH MTN MAP: Resolution Mountain
USGS MAPS: Vail Pass, Red Cliff, Pando

This alternate route could be considered the most direct line to the Fowler/Hilliard Hut, given weather good enough for 2 miles of ridge-running.

ROUTE DESCRIPTION: Start from the Vail Pass Trailhead. Put your skins on and, instead of skiing the Shrine Pass Road, ski S across West Tenmile Creek, then take a climbing traverse S then SW into Wilder Gulch. Ski about 3 miles and 1,165 vertical feet up Wilder Gulch to Ptarmigan Pass (11,765 feet). In general, the ski route follows the timber on the left side of the valley to about 11,200 feet. Here you swing W, then back S to Ptarmigan Pass. The USGS map shows the trail passing through a clearing at the saddle between the Wearyman and Wilder drainages. You need not ski the exact trail as long as you're careful about reaching Ptarmigan Pass, a broad saddle at 11,765 feet.

From Ptarmigan Pass ascend the east ridge of Ptarmigan Hill. At the summit of Ptarmigan Hill (12,143 feet), you'll find a good view and some wooden shacks that cover antennae. Descend the west face of Ptarmigan Hill to the saddle at 11,580 feet. This can be a fun little ski run, but may have some difficult snow. Remember, "there is no such thing as bad snow — just poor skiers".

From the saddle, follow a road cut that contours through sparse timber around the south side of point 11,683, then leads to the 11,480-foot saddle where you converge with route 9.5/8.4. Continue 1/3 mile W and SW along the ridge to the Fowler/Hilliard Hut. The hut is not visible until you top a small, 40-foot high hill several hundred feet E of the hut.

REVERSE ROUTE DESCRIPTION: Follow reverse route 9.3 from the Fowler/Hilliard Hut to Ptarmigan Pass. From Ptarmigan Pass, descend Wilder Gulch NE to about 10,600 feet, then traverse N out of Wilder Gulch, cross West Tenmile Creek, and continue N to the Vail Pass Trailhead.

SAFETY NOTES: Make prudent variations to avoid avalanche paths on the southeast-facing slopes of Wilder Gulch.

SUMMER: This is a fine hike or horse ride. Cyclists will have to shoulder their bikes to get up Wilder Gulch.

9.7
Fowler/Hilliard Hut to Shrine Mountain Inn via Shrine Mountain Ridge

DIFFICULTY: Intermediate
TIME: 5 1/2 hours
DISTANCE: 6 3/4 miles
ELEVATION GAIN: 930 feet; elevation loss: 1,221 feet
10TH MTN MAP: Resolution Mountain
USGS MAPS: Pando, Red Cliff, Vail Pass

This is the shortest 10th Mountain suggested route from the Fowler/Hilliard Hut to the Shrine Mountain Inn. It is scenic and a challenge to those who have just reached "intermediate status" with wilderness skiing.

ROUTE DESCRIPTION: From the front steps of the Fowler/Hilliard Hut, ski several hundred feet NE through sparse timber, then drop a short distance to a timbered saddle at 11,480 feet. From here follow a distinct snow-covered logging road down into the Wearyman Creek drainage. Novice downhillers can relax on the low-angled switchbacks of this road. Experts can ski the glades between the switchbacks. In either case, be sure you are on the road when it makes a last switchback at 11,240 feet, then heads E/NE on a low-angled traverse 1 ½ miles to road's end at 10,880 feet. Leave the road here and continue NE on a marked 10th Mountain trail that descends through dense timber to a small clearing in the creek bottom at 10,830 feet. Continue NE through the clearing, then climb a short steep hill up into the elongated park at 11,000 feet.

Cross to the north side of the park, put your skins on, and climb E then NW to 11,700 feet (timber line) on the west face of Shrine Mountain Ridge. Next, take a strict traverse 1 ½ miles across the west face to Shrine Mountain Saddle (11,740 feet, the saddle just SE of Shrine Mountain). This traverse passes through sparse timber and clearings at timber line.

At the north end of Shrine Mountain Saddle, use your map and compass to get your exact travel direction. Next, you should look at the cornices and develop a safe strategy for egress from the saddle. Drop down the northeast side of the saddle, and immediately you'll find an obvious trough. On the east side of this trough, you'll find the marked 10th Mountain suggested route. The blue diamonds take you along the east side of the trough for several hundred yards, then NE one mile to the Shrine Mountain Inn.

SAFETY NOTES: This route includes almost two miles of timber-line travel, where wind chill can make you wish for the sauna at the Inn, and poor visibility can break the best navigator. On the northeast side of Shrine Mountain Saddle take care to avoid any threatening, wind-loaded slopes under the cornices. This is done by remaining on the small ridge E of the aforementioned trough.

SUMMER: This route is a fine hike. A short section of trail, connecting Wearyman Creek with the logging road to the SW, is just a marked route through the forest with tread. Cyclists will enjoy all the roads in the area. Shrine Mountain Ridge is too high and rough for equestrian traffic, but the roads and "real" trails in the area are fine horse routes.

9.8

Fowler/Hilliard Hut to Shrine Mountain Inn via Wearyman Creek Road and Shrine Pass Road

DIFFICULTY: Advanced
TIME: 13 hours
DISTANCE: 14 miles
ELEVATION GAIN: 2,379 feet; elevation loss: 2,670 feet
10TH MTN MAP: Resolution Mountain
USGS MAPS: Pando, Red Cliff, Vail Pass

A storm howls at the Fowler/Hilliard Hut — you need to ski to the Shrine Mountain Inn. The bleak option of timber-line travel on route 9.6 is pushing you into a grand funk. What do you do? Use this alternate route. It's long and indirect, but safe in a storm. The route is rated advanced because of it's length.

ROUTE DESCRIPTION: Take 10th Mountain suggested route 9.7 to the 11,000-foot elongated park at Wearyman Creek. Leave route 9.7 here and ski to the far west end of the elongated park, where you'll find the distinct cut of the Wearyman Creek Road. Ski this road 4 miles down the valley to the Shrine Pass Road (9,000 feet).

In general, you turn E on the Shrine Pass Road and ski the road 5 miles up-valley to Shrine Pass. In detail: At 4 miles (from 9,000 feet), in a large clear area (10,320 feet), you hit the only switchback on the road. In poor weather, there is the possibility of losing the road here, especially with high winds. Just remember that the road leaves the gut of the drainage and climbs E through the clearing (staying on the north side of the drainage). The important thing is to find the road as it re-enters timber at the east end of the clearing, otherwise you'll have to beat some dense timber and brush.

Just ¼ mile into the timber (10,660 feet) you'll pass the left (N) turn-off of the Lime Creek Road (see route 8.2). Stay on the Shrine Pass Road and continue E then SE through light timber to Shrine Pass, a nondescript, flat clearing that forms the divide between Turkey Creek and West Tenmile Creek. Ski to the east end of the Shrine Pass clearing. Look for a White River National Forest sign facing E. Ski W from this sign several hundred yards across a clear area and enter a conifer forest at a red stock gate. Follow an obvious road cut through the forest ¼ mile S to the Shrine Mountain Inn. Use your map, compass, and altimeter for insurance. The large inn is visible from several hundred feet down the road.

SAFETY NOTES: Be sure to stay on the Shrine Pass Road, as there are several tempting turn-offs along the way. Don't let the ease of following this road lull you into complacent routefinding—use your skills. The Shrine Pass Road is heavily used by snowmobiles, so keep your eyes and ears open, and be courteous.

SUMMER: This route would be a fine horse ride or hike. Cyclists will enjoy the Wearyman Creek Road. To do the whole route on a bike, you'd have to portage the short section of 10th Mountain marked trail that connects SW from the elongated park to the upper road.

9.9

Fowler/Hilliard Hut to Schuss/Zesiger Hut via High Route

DIFFICULTY: Expert
TIME: 7 hours
DISTANCE: 6 ½ miles
ELEVATION GAIN: 2,282 feet; elevation loss: 2,122 feet
10TH MTN MAP: Chicago Ridge
USGS MAP: Pando

This alternate route to the Schuss/Zesiger Hut will give you more downhill skiing and better views than the Pearl Creek route (9.10). It is unmarked and includes several miles above timber line. Thus, you should spend plenty of time with your map, compass, and altimeter.

ROUTE DESCRIPTION: From the Fowler/Hilliard Hut, ski the 10th Mountain marked trail ¼ mile E and NE to the 11,480-foot saddle. Leave the 10th Mountain suggested route and continue SE on a distinct road cut that traverses ¾ mile through timber along the southwest side of point 11,683. At the south shoulder of point 11,683 (Ptarmigan Shoulder) cut a dropping traverse a short distance E, then enjoy a downhill run to Resolution Road at 10,704 feet.

Put your skins on, and get your map out. Leave Resolution Road and ski S across Resolution Creek, S up a shoulder, then traverse into the south fork of Resolution Creek. Cross the creek at about 10,800 feet, then climb to the head of the south Resolution Creek drainage to a distinct saddle (11,700 feet) E of point 11,860. Drop down the south side of the saddle to tree line in the north fork of Pearl Creek. Stay high and hold a traverse S above 11,400 feet to point 11,610 on the ridge between the two Pearl Creek drainages.

Once you crest the ridge, strip your skins and enjoy a 1,050-foot downhill SW into Pearl Creek, where you intersect 10th Mountain suggested route 9.10, which you then follow 2 miles up to the Schuss/Zesiger Hut.

SAFETY NOTES: This is an unmarked, high-altitude route with almost 2,000 vertical feet of steep downhill skiing. Take care with slide danger on the north and south sides of the 11,700-foot saddle and below the 11,400-foot traverse.

SUMMER: This route is not recommended for summer travel. If you want a summer high route (for hiking), try the Eagle/Summit county line.

9.10
Fowler/Hilliard Hut to Schuss/Zesiger Hut via Pearl Creek

DIFFICULTY: Intermediate
TIME: 8 hours
DISTANCE: 8 miles (1 ¾ mile less via Resolution Bowl)
ELEVATION GAIN: 2,238 feet; elevation loss: 2,078 feet
10TH MTN MAP: Chicago Ridge
USGS MAP: Pando

This roundabout 10th Mountain suggested route includes a scenic traverse of Resolution Mountain. For a more direct line with more downhill skiing, experts should consider skiing down Resolution Bowl from the front porch of the hut. This option puts you at about 10,400 feet on the Resolution Road, which you ski a mile downvalley to intersect the 10th Mountain suggested route described below. Only experts should make the complete descent of Resolution Bowl, as it necks down to steep, dense timber near the bottom. Lower down, the east side of the bowl is better than the west.

ROUTE DESCRIPTION: To take the 10th Mountain suggested route, follow route 9.2 from the Fowler/Hilliard Hut over the northwest shoulder of Resolution Mountain and down to Resolution Road. Ski one mile down Resolution Road to 9,678 feet (Pearl Creek/Resolution Creek confluence). From here you leave Resolution Road and climb the Pearl Creek drainage.

In detail: Turn left (SE) off Resolution Road onto another distinct road cut that takes a bridge across Resolution Creek. Once on the south side of the creek, look for a 10th Mountain marked trail that leaves the road cut and heads directly into the Pearl Creek drainage. Follow this trail for 1 ¾ miles on the southwest side of the creek to 10,320 feet, where you cross to the northeast side of the drainage and climb another ½ mile to 10,560 feet.

At 10,560 feet you're still deep in the Pearl Creek drainage, with the Schuss/Zesiger Hut above you to the SW. To reach it, make a 90-degree turn right (S) and climb the south side of the Pearl Creek drainage to the 11,420-foot saddle on the ridge between Pearl Creek and the East Fork of the Eagle River. This section of trail passes through intermittent clearings.

From the saddle, stick to the ridge and ski ¾ mile to the open clearing at the highest point on the ridge (11,716 feet), then drop SW to the Schuss/Zesiger Hut (11,660 feet) which sits just below and to the S of the highest part of the ridge. The building is visible from several hundred feet away, but you can miss it if you are skiing on the north side of the wide ridge crest, especially in a whiteout. If you know how long it takes you to ski ¾ mile, and you use your altimeter, you'll be sure to find it. Lazy mountaineers should look sharp!

SAFETY NOTES: Take care on the downhill into Resolution Creek. There can be slide danger in Resolution Bowl, both from large slab releases and small bank sluffs. Use proper precautions; stay on top of your orienteering.

SUMMER: You can hike down Resolution Bowl, but it'll make your knees hurt. The 10th Mountain recommended route is best for hiking, but the downhill into Resolution Creek is too rough for horses and bikes. For cyclists going to the Schuss/Zesiger from the Fowler/Hilliard, ride around Ptarmigan Hill to Resolution Road (see route 9.3). Descend Resolution Road to Camp Hale, then take Ranch Creek (see route 10.2) up to the Schuss/Zesiger Hut.

9.11

Resolution Mountain from Fowler/Hilliard Hut

DIFFICULTY: Intermediate to Expert
TIME: Several hours to a full day round trip
DISTANCE: ¾ mile round trip for summit of Resolution Mountain
ELEVATION GAIN: 405 feet to summit of Resolution Mountain
10TH MTN MAP: Chicago Ridge
USGS MAP: Pando

Rising to the SW of the Fowler/Hilliard Hut, Resolution Mountain is the only alpine terrain close to the hut. Skiing from the summit, you can find runs at almost all points of the compass. Beware of cornices, especially to the N and E of the summit. The wind can make poor snow conditions in the summit area, so explore lower down if you have trouble making turns.

ROUTE DESCRIPTION: To climb to the summit of Resolution Mountain, simply follow the northeast ridge from the Fowler/Hilliard Hut. Be careful with the cornices. One of the finest expert runs is a 1,000 vertical foot drop into Resolution Bowl (the bowl below the hut). The bottom portion of this bowl has quite a bit of brush, and the snow can be poor. You're best off skiing the bowl partway down, then skinning back up to the hut. If the southeast slopes have breakable crust, move around to the W or N.

All abilities will find good powder skiing in the glades down the hill NE of the hut. Ski in such a way as to intersect the lower switchback of the logging road which ascends to the hut from the Wearyman Creek drainage (see routes 9.5 and 8.4), then follow the logging road back up to the hut. There is also good glade skiing between the switchbacks on the logging road. If you have skins, it is more efficient to cut the switchbacks on the climb back up. Another good bet for intermediates and advanced skiers are the slopes of Ptarmigan Hill (see route 9.3). Again, be careful of avalanche slopes and try to use the exposure with the best snow.

SAFETY NOTES: Any of the open slopes on Resolution Mountain are potential slide areas. If you lack avalanche safety skills, stick to the glade skiing N of the hut.

SUMMER: The short walk to the summit of Resolution Mountain is a fine hike. It's a bit steep for all but the "extreme equestrian". Cyclists should leave their rigs at the hut.

9.12

Ptarmigan Hill from the Fowler/Hilliard Hut

DIFFICULTY: Intermediate
TIME: 3 1/2 hours round trip
DISTANCE: 4 miles round trip
ELEVATION GAIN: 683 feet round trip
10TH MTN MAP: Resolution Mountain or Chicago Ridge
USGS MAP: Pando

Many skiers would rather explore the peaks than practice their turns. If you feel that way, do this tour.

ROUTE DESCRIPTION: The route is simple – it follows the ridge leading E from the hut 2 miles to the summit of Ptarmigan Hill. For details see route 9.3

SAFETY NOTES: Remember that this route is mostly at or above timber line. See route 9.3.

SUMMER: This is a fine hike. Horses and cyclists should stick to the road that traverses along the south side of the ridge and intersects the Resolution Road at 11,360 feet.

Chapter 10 • Schuss/Zesiger Hut

Located near timber line, the Schuss/Zesiger Hut has good local skiing and terrific views of several 14,000-foot peaks. The hut is owned by 10th Mountain and conforms to 10th Mountain's basic hut specifications. It is almost identical to the Fowler/Hilliard Hut.

ELEVATION:	11,660 feet
COUNTY:	Eagle
TEXT MAP:	pp. 138-139
10TH MTN MAP:	Chicago Ridge
USGS MAP:	Pando
TRAILHEADS:	Pando, S. Camp Hale

As is the case with several other huts the Leadville area, the Schuss/Zesiger Hut is very close to a trailhead. While this can make trailhead to hut skiing less appealing to an experienced skier, it is a boon for those at the learning stage. Fortunately, there is plenty of base skiing you can do from the Schuss/Zesiger, so consider carrying a few days supplies in from the trailhead for branch skiing from the hut.

The Schuss/Zesiger Hut was built with money donated by Jack Schuss and Al Zesiger, two strong supporters of 10th Mountain. Their example should serve to remind us all that the 10th Mountain huts exist soley because of countless monetary donations and volunteer work hours.

The quickest trailhead to hut route to the Schuss/Zesiger Hut is the Ranch Creek route (10.2). For ski-throughs N to the Fowler/Hilliard Hut, you can choose between an alternate high route (10.4) or a 10th Mountain suggested route (10.5) that sticks more to the valleys, but still hits timber line. For a ski-through south to Vance's Cabin, use route 10.6. You won't come continued on pp. 110-111

10th Mountain Hut & Trail System

10th Mountain Trail is located in the White River and San Isabel National Forests under agreement with the Forest Service, USDA.

Scale 1:24,000

SCALE IN MILES

0   .25   .50   .75   1

● Hut
● Trailhead

MN 12°

Trails are marked by blue diamonds, except in wilderness areas where trails are marked by tree blazes. It is just not a substitute for good route finding skills, a good map and the ability to locate roads.

This map is not a substitute for good route finding skills, it is just not a substitute for good route finding skills.

These are suggested routes only.

Trails are not groomed and their exact location may vary.

© 1989 - 10th Mountain Trail Association

SAN ISABEL NATIONAL FOREST

Ptarmigan Pass

Ptarmigan Hills

9.3

To Shrine Mountain Inn
0.30 miles to Fowler/Hilliard Hut
6.49 miles to Shrine Mountain Inn

9.3
9.6

9.9
10.4

9.12

Resolution Narrows

Fowler/Hilliard Hut
11,500'

Ptarmigan Shoulder

9.11

9.3

Resolution Mountain

1.10 miles to Fowler/Hilliard Hut
3.91 miles to Pando
5.34 miles to Camp Hale
6.71 miles to Schuss/Zeisiger Hut

2.82 miles to Fowler/Hilliard Hut
3.02 miles to Camp Hale
4.99 miles to Schuss/Zeisiger Hut

9.9
10.4

1.86 miles to Schuss/Zeisiger Hut
4.76 miles to Camp Hale
5.95 miles to Fowler/Hilliard Hut

9.10
10.1
10.5

0.50 miles to Fowler/Hilliard Hut
4.51 miles to Pando
5.94 miles to Schuss/Zeisiger Hut
7.31 miles to Camp Hale
6.48 miles to Red Cliff

9.4

Hornsilver Mountain

9.1

9.10
10.5

2.02 miles to Camp Hale
2.82 miles to Fowler/Hilliard Hut
3.98 miles to Schuss/Zeisiger Hut

Pearl Creek

3.01 miles to Camp Hale
3.50 miles to Fowler/Hilliard Hut via Resolution Creek
4.60 miles to Fowler/Hilliard Hut via McAllister Gulch

9.10
10.1
10.5

Schuss/Zeisiger Hut
11,660'

9.2
9.3
10.1

.76 miles to Pando
4.29 miles to Fowler/Hilliard Hut

Resolution Road

Gravel Pit

.22 miles to Camp Hale
5.92 miles to Fowler/Hilliard Hut
5.39 miles to Schuss/Zeisiger Hut
5.60 miles to Fowler/Hilliard Hut

0.47 miles to Camp Hale

Resolution Creek

10.2

10.7

0.60 miles to Schuss/Zeisiger Hut
5.98 miles to Camp Hale via Resolution Creek
6.18 miles to Camp Hale via Cataract Creek
7.18 miles to Fowler/Hilliard Hut
7.92 miles to Vance's Cabin

1.55 miles to Schuss/Zeisiger Hut
5.28 miles to Camp Hale

10.3

JEEP TRAIL

Cataract Creek

Ranch Creek

Pando Trailhead
9,800

Camp Hale (Site)

Gravel Pits

Eagle River

CAMP HALE

Camp Hale Trailhead
9,260

South Camp Hale

AND

DENVER

To Red Cliff

McAllister

Searle Gulch

Searle

Searle Pass

Corbett Peak

Elk Mtn

Sugarloaf Peak

Pearl Peak

Kokomo Pass

North

WHITE RIVER

NATIONAL FOREST

10.6
11.1
11.3

2.19 miles to Vance's Cabin
6.43 miles to Schuss/Zeiger Hut
6.52 miles to Camp Hale

2.77 miles to Vance's Cabin
5.78 miles to Schuss/Zeiger Hut
5.87 miles to Camp Hale

1.33 miles to Vance's Cabin
7.22 miles to Schuss/Zeiger Hut
7.31 miles to Camp Hale

0.71 miles to Vance's Cabin
7.84 miles to Schuss/Zeiger Hut
7.93 miles to Camp Hale

11.5

0.28 miles to Vance's Cabin
2.84 miles to Tennessee Pass

11.6

1.06 miles to Tennessee Pass
2.06 miles to Vance's Cabin

Vance's Cabin
10,980'

11.2
11.4
12.4

1.46 miles to Vance's Cabin
1.66 miles to Tennessee Pass

Tennessee Pass Trailhead
10,424'

Ski Cooper/Ski Area

11.4
12.4

Crane Park
Trailhead
10,137'

12.2

This map includes U.S. Forest Service
trails that do not conform to present
10th Mountain Trail   standards.

continued on pp. 158-159(?)

139

across much alpine ski mountaineering near the Schuss/Zesiger Hut, but you'll find plenty of powder skiing in local glades.

10.1
Pando Trailhead — Schuss/Zesiger Hut via Pearl Creek

DIFFICULTY: Intermediate
TIME: 8 hours up, 6 hours down
DISTANCE: 7 1/4 miles
ELEVATION GAIN: 2,516 feet; elevation loss 56 feet
10TH MTN MAP: Chicago Ridge
USGS MAP: Pando

This 10th Mountain suggested route is the longest trail to the Schuss/Zesiger Hut. Most often the Pearl Creek section is used as part of the ski-through between the Schuss/Zesiger and Fowler/Hilliard huts.

ROUTE DESCRIPTION: From the Pando Trailhead ski E across the main north/south Camp Hale Road, across a bridge over the Eagle River, then E and NE to intersect a snow-covered road running N/S at the base of the mountain. Ski this road N a short distance, then turn right and ski SE up through a gulch E of point 9,540 (this is not the main Camp Hale Road). One mile from Pando you intersect the distinct Resolution Road. Take a left (NE) and ski 1 1/2 miles up the Resolution Road to 9,678 feet.

Turn right (SE) off the Resolution Road onto another distinct road cut that crosses a bridge over Resolution Creek. Once on the south side of the creek, look for a 10th Mountain marked trail that leaves the road cut and heads directly into the Pearl Creek drainage. Follow this trail for 1 3/4 miles on the southwest side of the creek to 10,320 feet where you cross to the northeast side of the drainage and climb another 1/2 mile to 10,560 feet.

At 10,560 feet you're still deep in the Pearl Creek drainage, with the Schuss/Zesiger Hut high above you to the SW. To get there make a 90-degree turn and climb through willows and clearings to 11,000 feet, then out of Pearl Creek to an 11,420-foot saddle on the ridge between Pearl Creek and the East Fork of the Eagle River.

From the saddle, stick to the ridge and ski 3/4 mile to the open clearing at the highest point on the ridge (11,716 feet), then drop SW to the Schuss/Zesiger Hut (11,660 feet) which sits just below and to the S of the highest part of the ridge. The building is visible from several hundred feet away, but you can miss it if you are skiing on the north side of the wide ridge crest, especially in a whiteout. If you know how long it takes you to ski 3/4 mile and you use your altimeter, you'll be sure to find it.

REVERSE ROUTE DESCRIPTION: From the front steps of the Schuss/Zesiger Hut, traverse NE several hundred feet to the ridge crest. Descend the ridge E ¾ mile to the distinct 11,420-foot saddle. Drop down the north side of the saddle into Pearl Creek. You can get in some turns for a few hundred vertical feet, but make sure you're on the 10th Mountain marked trail when the willows begin, otherwise you'll "wander in the willows".

Intersect Pearl Creek at 10,560 feet and cross to the north side of the creck. Descend the Pearl Creek drainage to Resolution Road in the Resolution Creek drainage.

Ski Resolution Road SW two miles downvalley to Camp Hale. For the Pando Trailhead, take a right just before you make a final short drop into the flats of Camp Hale and ski N on a road tucked in behind point 9,540. Just N of point 9,540 you'll intersect a main north/south snow-covered road. Take a left (S) here, turn W, and ski across the flats to a bridge over the Eagle River. The Pando Trailhead is several hundred feet W of the bridge.

If visibility is poor in Camp Hale you might have trouble finding the Pando Trailhead and bridge. In this case you can strike cross country to Highway 24, your only obstacles being the Eagle River and up to a mile of trail to break out. In midwinter there usually are snow bridges over the Eagle River.

SAFETY NOTES: Use your survival ski skills on the descent from the 11,420-foot saddle.

SUMMER: Hikers and equestrians will enjoy this route.

10.2

South Camp Hale Trailhead — Schuss/Zesiger Hut via Ranch Creek

DIFFICULTY: Intermediate
TIME: 4 ¾ hours up, 3 hours down
DISTANCE: 3 ⅛ miles
ELEVATION GAIN: 2,436 feet; elevation loss: 56 feet
10TH MTN MAP: Chicago Ridge
USGS MAP: Pando

This trailhead to hut route is short and to the point. It is a 10th Mountain suggested route, and uses a portion of the popular snowmobile trail in Camp Hale; so keep an open ear and nimble feet.

ROUTE DESCRIPTION: From the South Camp Hale Trailhead, ski NE across the flats of Camp Hale (use a snow bridge to cross the Eagle River, as there is no bridge here). Intersect the road at the base of the mountain, turn right (SE), and ski the snow-covered road ¼ mile to the well-signed intersection with the Ranch Creek Road.

Put on your skins here. Take a left (N) on the **Ranch Creek Road** and follow a distinct road cut that climbs Ranch Creek 2 miles to 10,700 feet. Here you'll break into a clearing with several beautiful old cabins. Climb NE through the clearing and re-enter the timber at about 10,900 feet. Follow the trail up several switchbacks. Strong skiers will certainly want to cut some of these switchbacks. If you do so, take care to relocate the 10th Mountain marked trail.

At 11,220 feet the trail takes an important right turn (E), then climbs ¼ mile (around 2 more switchbacks) to a large open area on the ridge. Follow the ridge E ½ mile to the ridge top at 11,716 feet. As you are skiing along the flat, sparsely timbered ridge top, you'll see the stove pipes of the hut down to your right. In poor visibility take care not to overshoot the hut. Your altimeter can help prevent this, since the main goal is the high point of the ridge. Ski a few hundred feet E along the ridge top, then double back W to the hut.

REVERSE ROUTE DESCRIPTION: From the front steps of the hut, take a climbing traverse NE to the ridge crest, then head W over the ridge top. Stick to the broad ridge crest for ½ mile, then drop W into the Ranch Creek drainage on a marked 10th Mountain suggested route. If you're an expert, you can cut most of the switchbacks on the marked trail and enjoy turns down the fall line in the clearing beginning at about 10,900 feet. Be sure to intersect the road cut at the lower edge of a clearing. The road down the Ranch Creek drainage is easy to follow. At the flats of Camp Hale use your map to reach the South Camp Hale Trailhead. If a whiteout cuts the view, just strike out across the flats on a compass bearing and you'll hit Highway 24. If you're really good, you should be able to follow a bearing to within a few feet of the trailhead.

SAFETY NOTES: This trail begins as one of those "nose to the grindstone" climbs. However, the last part of the route (on the ridge) requires some attention.

SUMMER: The Ranch Creek Road is a good bike, horse, and cycle route. It does not connect to the hut, but cyclists can easily manage the short portage.

10.3

South Camp Hale Trailhead — Schuss/Zesiger Hut via Cataract Creek

DIFFICULTY: Intermediate
TIME: 5 1/2 hours up, 4 hours down
DISTANCE: 5 1/3 miles
ELEVATION GAIN: 2,436 feet; elevation loss: 56 feet
10TH MTN MAP: Chicago Ridge
USGS MAP: Pando

This is the "medium length" trailhead to hut route for the Schuss/Zesiger Hut. It is more useful as a descent on the route to Vance's Cabin (see route 10.6).

ROUTE DESCRIPTION: Start at the South Camp Hale Trailhead, with waxed skis. Ski NE across the flats of Camp Hale (find a snow bridge to cross the Eagle River). Intersect the road at the base of the mountain, turn right (SE), and ski the snow-covered road 2 1/4 miles up the flat drainage of the East Fork of the Eagle River. Put your skins on here and take a left (9,560 feet) onto the Cataract Creek jeep trail. From here you climb the jeep trail. The Colorado Trail uses the Cataract Creek jeep trail, so you'll find the little triangular Colorado Trail markers along with standard 10th Mountain markers. Cataract Creek is nestled in a steep-sided gulch, so the road winds as it works its way through the gulch. At 10,720 feet in the Cataract Creek drainage you leave the jeep trail and climb N 1/2 mile to a wide saddle (11,420 feet) atop the north ridge of the drainage.

Ski W from the saddle, over a bump, to another 11,420-foot saddle (intersection with route 10.1). From here, stick to the ridge and ski 3/4 mile W to the open clearing at the highest point on the ridge (11,716 feet), then drop S to the Schuss/Zesiger Hut (11,660 feet) which sits just below and to the S of the highest part of the ridge. The building is visible from several hundred feet away, but you can miss it if you are skiing on the north side of the wide ridge crest, especially in a whiteout.

REVERSE ROUTE DESCRIPTION: From the front steps of the Schuss/Zesiger Hut, traverse NE several hundred feet to the ridge crest. Descend the ridge E 3/4 mile to the distinct 11,420-foot saddle dividing the Eagle River and Pearl Creek drainages. Continue SE from the saddle, traversing around the south side of point 11,475 to another 11,420-foot saddle. Drop S from here into the Cataract Creek drainage, and intersect the Cataract Creek jeep trail at 10,720 feet. Descend the jeep trail to the valley floor of the Eagle River drainage, then follow the main, snow-covered road W downvalley to the trailhead.

SAFETY NOTES: For the most part, the Cataract Creek jeep trail keeps you out of a steep-sided gulch. One section of the road, however, from 10,360 feet down to the creek crossing at 10,160 feet, would take you under a dangerous, steep bank. You bypass this to the E on a short 10th Mountain route with standard markings.

SUMMER: The Cataract Creek jeep trail is a fine bicycle route, but you have to portage from the jeep trail to the ridge. Hikers and horse people will enjoy this whole route.

10.4

Schuss/Zesiger Hut to Fowler/Hilliard Hut via High Route

DIFFICULTY: Expert
TIME: 8 hours
DISTANCE: 6 ½ miles
ELEVATION GAIN: 2,122 feet; elevation loss: 2,282 feet
10TH MTN MAP: Chicago Ridge
USGS MAP: Pando

This alternate route to the Schuss/Zesiger Hut will give you more downhill skiing and better views than the Pearl Creek route (9.10). It is unmarked and includes several miles above timber line. Thus, you should put plenty of time into using your map, compass, and altimeter.

ROUTE DESCRIPTION: From the Schuss/Zesiger Hut, follow 10th Mountain suggested reverse route 10.1 to 10,560 feet in Pearl Creek. Leave the marked trail and climb N up the side of the drainage to point 11,610. Pass to the right (E) of point 11,610 and cut a high traverse through the bowl at the head of the north fork of Pearl Creek. Climb the north side of the bowl about 200 vertical feet to a distinct saddle (11,700 feet).

From the saddle, descend the south fork of Resolution Creek (use the south side of the drainage) to 10,800 feet. Cross the creek here and cut a traverse N out of the drainage. This avoids a gulch lower down and saves you some elevation. Take a short drop into Resolution Creek, cross the creek, and gain the obvious Resolution Road at 10,704 feet.

From here you use the Ptarmigan Shoulder route (see route 9.3). Leave the road and ski N up the east side of an intermittent stream in a gulch. At 11,000 feet take a climbing traverse W to the ridge (Ptarmigan Shoulder) leading up to point 11,683. Ascend the ridge to the road cut that contours through sparse timber around the southwest side of 11,683. Follow this road W. It will take you to the 11,480-foot saddle where you converge with route 9.5/8.4. From here continue ⅓ mile W and SW along the ridge to the

Fowler/Hilliard Hut. The hut is not visible until you top a small, 40-foot high hill several hundred feet E of the hut.

SAFETY NOTES: The high traverse in the north fork of Pearl Creek avoids steeper slopes below. Even so, there could be some slide danger here. Remember that this is an unmarked, expert route.

SUMMER: This route is fine for an "off-trail" hike. Equestrians and cyclists should stick to the roads and maintained trails.

10.5

Schuss/Zesiger Hut to Fowler/Hilliard Hut via Pearl Creek

DIFFICULTY: Intermediate
TIME: 8 hours
DISTANCE: 8 miles
ELEVATION GAIN: 2,078 feet; elevation loss: 2,238 feet
10TH MTN MAP: Chicago Ridge
USGS MAP: Pando

This is a basic ski-through route. It uses marked 10th Mountain suggested routes and includes some scenic timber-line travel.

ROUTE DESCRIPTION: From the front steps of the Schuss/Zesiger Hut, traverse NE several hundred feet to the ridge crest. Descend the ridge E ¾ mile to the distinct 11,420-foot saddle. Drop down the north side of the saddle into Pearl Creek. You can get in some turns for a few hundred vertical feet, but make sure you're on the 10th Mountain marked trail when the willows begin, otherwise you'll have to "beat the rushes".

Intersect Pearl Creek at 10,560 feet and cross to the north side of the creek (route 9.9/10.4 intersects here). Descend the Pearl Creek drainage 2 ⅛ miles to the Resolution Creek drainage. Cross a bridge over Resolution Creek and gain the distinct cut of the Resolution Road.

Ski the Resolution Road 1 mile upvalley to 9,960 feet. Leave the Resolution Road here and take a left (NW) onto a marked 10th Mountain trail. The blue diamonds take you up to a 10,940-foot saddle on the southwest ridge of Resolution Mountain. Most of this trail follows a distinct trail cut through forest. In the occasional clearing, take the time to really zero in on the route with your map. Remember: diamonds are for dummies.

Climb the southwest ridge of Resolution Mountain ¾ mile to 11,400 feet (you'll pass the intersection of route 9.1 at 11,300 feet). Next, take a ¾-mile climbing traverse NE then N across the west face of Resolution

Mountain, ending at 11,700-foot Resolution Saddle on the northwest ridge of Resolution Mountain. Ski down E from the saddle and cut a short traverse that leads to a distinct E/W cleft called the Resolution Narrows. Take care not to ski N downhill from the saddle. Continue E down the cleft to the Fowler/Hilliard Hut in a clearing at 11,500 feet. In clear weather the hut is visible from Resolution Saddle. To get some "bonus turns", experts should consider ascending Resolution Mountain, then cutting turns down to the hut.

SAFETY NOTES: There can be slide danger on the open slopes of Resolution Mountain. Be aware of cornices on all the ridges. The trails out of Camp Hale are often used by snowmobiles.

SUMMER: This route is not recommended for hiking. The section of trail from Resolution Creek climbing to Resolution Mountain is a marked ski route with no foot path for horse or bike travel. The Resolution Road is a good bicycle route.

10.6
Schuss/Zesiger Hut to Vance's Cabin via Cataract Creek

DIFFICULTY: Intermediate
TIME: 7 hours
DISTANCE: 8 ½ miles
ELEVATION GAIN: 1,420 feet; elevation loss: 2,100 feet
10TH MTN MAP: Chicago Ridge
USGS MAP: Pando

This 10th Mountain suggested route is the standard ski-through route from the Schuss/Zesiger Hut to Vance's Cabin.

ROUTE DESCRIPTION: From the front steps of the Schuss/Zesiger Hut, traverse NE several hundred feet to the ridge crest. Descend the ridge E ¾ mile to the distinct 11,420-foot saddle dividing the Eagle River and Pearl Creek drainages. Continue SE from the saddle over point 11,475 to another 11,420-foot saddle. Drop S from here into the Cataract Creek drainage and intersect the Cataract Creek jeep trail at 10,720 feet. Descend the jeep trail to the valley floor of the Eagle River drainage.

Follow a snow-covered main road ¼ mile upvalley. Just after the snow-covered road crosses the East Fork of the Eagle River (no bridge). Leave the main road here and ski right (S) several hundred feet across a flat area. Swing SW and begin a climbing traverse that leads up a marked trail cut two miles through timber to Jones Gulch. Stay on the northeast side of

Jones Creek and parallel the creek to a marshy clearing at the 10,400-foot level.

Follow the marked trail W along the north side of the clearing, then continue on a climbing traverse NW (on sections of road and trail) to 10,600 feet on a shoulder. Swing S and climb the shoulder to 11,033 feet. From here the trail leaves the crest of the shoulder and follows a long 1 1/2-mile-climbing traverse through medium density timber to the lower edge of a burn area at 11,000 feet on the west shoulder of Taylor Hill.

The hut sits at the lower southwest end of the burn on the side of a rise and is not too visible from where you enter the burn. However, there are some structures around the hut that you can see from a little farther away.

SAFETY NOTES: For the most part, the Cataract Creek jeep trail keeps you out of a steep-sided gulch. One section of the road, however, from 10,360 feet down to the creek crossing at 10,160 feet, would take you under a dangerous, steep bank. You bypass this to the E on a short 10th Mountain route with standard markings.

SUMMER: This is not a suitable summer route (see Chapter 11 for Vance's Cabin summer ideas).

On the ridge from the Schuss/Zesiger Hut to the Cataract Creek trail.

10.7

Day skiing from Schuss/Zesiger Hut

DIFFICULTY: Intermediate to Advanced
TIME: Several hours to half day
DISTANCE: Varies
ELEVATION GAIN: Varies
10TH MTN MAP: Chicago Ridge
USGS MAP: Pando

The Schuss/Zesiger Hut is located in the midst of some fine glade skiing.
You'll find slopes on all exposures, so move around to find the good snow.

ROUTE DESCRIPTION: One good run takes the open areas at the head of
Pearl Creek just W of the 10th Mountain suggested route. Cut over to the
trail as soon as the trees tighten and use the trail for your climb back up.
Be careful of small cliffs farther to the W.

You can also ski S from the front porch. Head down the open area, then
into trees that soon thicken into an unskiable forest. Enjoy a few laps.

You can get another good run by simply following the Ranch Creek route
(see route 10.2). Cut the switchbacks down to 11,000 feet, then make figure-
eights in the open area down to the forest. Do laps here until dinnertime.

SAFETY NOTES: By doing some exploring, you can find dozens of hidden
powder caches. If you go wild, make sure you have time to climb back to
the hut before dark. Beware of sudden drop-offs and cliff areas.

Skiing backcountry powder.

Chapter 11 • Vance's Cabin

Vance's Cabin is a privately owned hut located on a timbered mountainside near Tennessee Pass. Through compact, it sleeps 16. It has a gas stove, gas lights, refrigerator, and sauna. Reservations are taken by 10th Mountain. Construction of the cabin began in 1980 and was completed in 1988.

ELEVATION: 10,980 feet
COUNTY: Eagle
TEXT MAP: pp. 138-139, 158-159
10TH MTN MAP: Chi. Rdg., Galena Mt.
USGS MAP: Pando
TRAILHEADS: South Camp Hale, Tennessee Pass

The quick trail to Vance's Cabin is the Piney Gulch route (11.2). For ski-throughs use route 11.3 to head north, and route 11.4 to head south. Novice mountaineers will find good day trips on Taylor Hill to the east of the Cabin. Experts can explore Chicago Ridge farther to the east.

In the past, Vance's Cabin has been open in late summer and fall (as well as in winter). The best hike, bike, and horse route to the hut takes Piney Gulch (route 11.2). For cyclists, a short road route uses the road shown on the USGS map climbing from Highway 24 up past the El Capitan Mine, then up to the cabin. There is no parking at the start of this road. All the dirt roads and trails in the area are worth exploring. There is fine alpine hiking on Taylor Hill and farther east on Chicago Ridge.

The nearby town of Leadville (10,152 feet) is the highest city of it's size in the United States. Leadville is a charismatic old mining town created by the gold and silver boom in the late 1800s. Curiosity seekers will find several excellent museums and plenty of photographic old buildings. Lodging and dining in the old mining town are fun and affordable. Harrison Avenue is the main street through the old part of town. Here you'll find the fabulous restored Hotel Delaware, as well as several affordable motels. The ubiquitous Best Western is in the strip development on the north side of town. For dining, don't miss authentic mexican food at The Grill on the west end of Elm Street. For breakfast, try the Golden Rose and Golden Burro cafes on Harrison Avenue.

11.1

South Camp Hale Trailhead — Vance's Cabin via East Fork Eagle River

DIFFICULTY: Intermediate
TIME: 7 hours up, 5 hours down
DISTANCE: 8 miles
ELEVATION GAIN: 1,700 feet
10TH MTN MAP: Chicago Ridge
USGS MAPS: Pando

This 10th Mountain suggested route is the longer trailhead to hut route for Vance's Cabin. It serves most often as part of the ski-through route from the Schuss/Zesiger Hut, but it also makes a fine tour in it's own right.

ROUTE DESCRIPTION: From the South Camp Hale Trailhead, ski E across the flats of Camp Hale (no bridge across Eagle River). Intersect the snow-covered road at the base of the mountain (usually packed by snowmobile) and ski this road 2 ¼ miles up the East Fork of the Eagle River to 9,560 feet, just past a flat marshy area with a small pond. In winter this pond will be obscured by snow. Turn right (S) off the road just after you cross the East Fork of the Eagle River (no bridge). Continue S for several hundred feet across the flat area. Swing SW and begin a climbing traverse that leads up a marked trail cut 2 miles through timber to Jones Gulch. Stay on the northeast side of Jones Creek and parallel the creek to a marshy clearing at the 10,400-foot level.

Follow the marked trail W along the north side of the clearing, then continue on a climbing traverse NW (on sections of road and trail) to 10,600 feet on a shoulder. Swing S and climb the shoulder to 11,033 feet. From here the trail leaves the crest of the shoulder and follows a long 1 ½-mile climbing traverse through medium density timber to the lower edge of a burn area at 11,000 feet on the west shoulder of Taylor Hill.

The hut sits at the lower southwest end of the burn on the side of a rise and is not too visible from where you enter the burn. However, there are some structures around the hut that are easier to spot.

REVERSE ROUTE DESCRIPTION: From the front door of Vance's Cabin, ski N across a clearing. In the timber at the north end of the clearing take care to find the marked 10th Mountain trail that leads N from the clearing on a 1 ¼-mile traverse (on roads and trails) to 11,033 feet. From here continue N down the ridge ¾ mile to 10,600 feet.

Turn right (E) and follow another dropping traverse to a flat marshy clearing at 10,400 feet in Jones Gulch. Stick to the north edge of the clearing, cross Jones Creek, then descend N down the east side of Jones Gulch (can be a scary downhill). When the angle eases off at 10,220 feet, turn right (E) again and drop through several curves to a long easterly trail cut that takes you to the East Fork of the Eagle River.

Cross the Eagle River and ski the snow-covered road 2 ¾ miles downvalley to the South Camp Hale Trailhead. Take care not to overshoot the trailhead. Basically, when the road you skied NW (down the East Fork) turns N, take a hard left and ski SW across the flats of former Camp Hale ½ mile to the trailhead at Highway 24.

Experts can save a great deal of distance by continuing down the fall line from the turn at 11,600 feet. There is some dense timber on this route, so only experts should attempt it.

SAFETY NOTES: During storms, visibility in the flats of Camp Hale can be limited. Careful use of compass bearings can keep you on the correct path.

SUMMER: This trail is unsuitable for summer travel. Vance's Cabin may be open in the summer; check with 10th Mountain for the latest information. The dirt roads and trails in the area, however, are fine horse, bike, and hike routes.

11.2

Tennessee Pass Trailhead — Vance's Cabin via Piney Gulch

DIFFICULTY: Intermediate
TIME: 4 hours up, 3 hours down
DISTANCE: 3 1/8 miles
ELEVATION GAIN: 556 feet
10TH MTN MAP: Chicago Ridge
USGS MAPS: Leadville North, Pando

This is one of the shortest, easiest trailhead to hut routes in the whole 10th Mountain system. As such, it's a good "first hut" tour. But it still follows a backcountry trail, so be realistic. It is a 10th Mountain suggested route, but the standard 10th Mountain trail markings can be confused with the cross country trail markings (Ski Cooper Nordic trails) at the beginning of the route.

ROUTE DESCRIPTION: Begin at the Tennessee Pass Trailhead. From your parking on the west side of Highway 24, cross the highway and walk up the obvious road 1/2 mile E to the parking lot of Ski Cooper. You can ski on the north side of the road if walking is not to your taste.

Once in the parking lot, find the start of the Nordic trail system at the northeast corner of the lot next to the Nordic Center building. Follow the maintained Nordic trail NE along a water ditch that traverses into Piney Gulch. At 3/4 mile from the Nordic Center the gulch splits (10,520 feet). Leave the Nordic trail system here and ski up the left (N) fork of the gulch for 1/4 mile to a large clearing (10,660 feet).

Climb NW up through the clearing to the north end of the saddle N of point 10,963. At the saddle use your map and compass to identify the slopes of Taylor Hill. Climb to the E for a short distance, then swing back N and make a long 1/2-mile traverse along the west face of Taylor Hill. At 11,160 feet, just to the E of the hut, you enter an open area. Turn left here and descend 1/4 mile to Vance's Cabin. Some structures around the cabin are visible from several hundred yards.

REVERSE ROUTE DESCRIPTION: From the front door of Vance's Cabin ski N for 1/4 mile, then turn right (E) and climb to 11,160 feet on the west face of Taylor Hill. Turn right (S) and ski a level traverse 1/2 mile through timber, then drop S and W to the saddle N of point 10,963. You don't quite ski to the apex of the saddle. Instead, from the north end of the saddle, turn SE and drop through clearings to 10,660 feet in the north fork of Piney Gulch. Ski down the gulch a short distance, cross the creek and follow the east side of the creek to the confluence of the north and south forks of Piney Gulch. From here follow the Ski Cooper Nordic trail system to the Ski Cooper parking area. Take the Ski Cooper access road to the Tennessee Pass Trailhead. You can walk this road or ski next to it on the north side.

SAFETY NOTES: Don't let the short length of this route make you lazy.

SUMMER: This is the preferred summer route to Vance's Cabin.

11.3
Vance's Cabin to Schuss/Zesiger Hut via Cataract Creek

DIFFICULTY: Intermediate
TIME: 8 hours
DISTANCE: 8 ½ miles
ELEVATION GAIN: 2,156 feet; elevation loss: 1,476 feet
10TH MTN MAP: Chicago Ridge
USGS MAP: Pando

This 10th Mountain suggested route is the standard ski-through route from Vance's Cabin to the Schuss/Zesiger Hut. It includes a nice ridge crest and a fairly direct climb.

ROUTE DESCRIPTION: From Vance's Cabin, follow reverse route 11.1 down to the crossing of the East Fork of the Eagle River. Follow the snow-covered road (north side of valley) ¼ mile downvalley to the Cataract Creek jeep road. Turn right (N) and follow route 10.3 up the Cataract Creek jeep road and on to the Schuss/Zesiger Hut. The Colorado Trail uses the Cataract Creek jeep road, so you'll find the little triangular Colorado Trail markers along with standard 10th Mountain markers.

SAFETY NOTES: See notes on routes 10.3 and 11.1.

SUMMER: See notes on routes 10.3 and 11.1.

11.4

Vance's Cabin to 10th Mountain Division Hut via Tennessee Pass

DIFFICULTY: Intermediate
TIME: 9 hours
DISTANCE: 9 miles
ELEVATION GAIN: 1,150 feet; elevation loss: 760 feet
10TH MTN MAPS: Chicago Ridge and Galena Mountain
USGS MAPS: Pando, Leadville North, Homestake Reservoir

This 10th Mountain suggested route is the standard ski-through from Vance's Cabin to the 10th Mountain Division Hut. It passes Ski Cooper and crosses a major highway. Plan a resupply for the highway if you're on a long ski-through.

ROUTE DESCRIPTION: First take reverse route 11.2 to Tennessee Pass, then follow route 12.1 to the 10th Mountain Division Hut.

SAFETY NOTES: This is a long route, so start early. See notes for routes 11.2 and 12.1.

SUMMER: See notes for routes 11.2 and 12.1.

11.5

Taylor Hill from Vance's Cabin

DIFFICULTY: Intermediate
TIME: Several hours to half day round trip
DISTANCE: 1 ½ miles round trip
ELEVATION GAIN: 745 feet round trip
10TH MTN MAP: Chicago Ridge
USGS MAP: Pando

This branch route is a fine climb with plenty of ski options.

ROUTE DESCRIPTION: Put on your skins at the cabin. From the front door of Vance's Cabin ski N for ¼ mile (or a bit less), then turn right (E) and climb to 11,160 feet on the west face of Taylor Hill. At 11,160 feet, where the marked trail turns right (S), leave the trail and continue to climb E ½ mile to the summit of Taylor Hill (11,725 feet). For good skiing stay N of the ascent route and enjoy open slopes back down to the clearing just N of the cabin.

You can also find some glade skiing by dropping from the Taylor Hill summit S into Piney Gulch, then picking up route 11.2 back to the cabin. This is a more advanced option. If you want shorter runs, just play on the open slope behind the cabin.

SAFETY NOTES: Stay away from the steep north face of Taylor Hill and beware of cornices on the summit.

SUMMER: This is a fine alpine hike.

11.6

Chicago Ridge from Vance's Cabin

DIFFICULTY: Advanced
TIME: Full day round trip
DISTANCE: 4 ½ miles round trip
ELEVATION GAIN: 1,562 feet round trip
10TH MTN MAP: Chicago Ridge
USGS MAP: Pando

If you thought Taylor Hill was a mountain, wait until you see Chicago Ridge! This majestic crest winds for 5 miles along a north/south axis to the E of Vance's Cabin. If you were ambitious enough, you could gain the high point via this route, then ski the ridge S all the way to the outskirts of Leadville.

ROUTE DESCRIPTION: To climb from Vance's Cabin to the high point of the ridge, follow route 11.5 to the summit of Taylor Hill. As you'll see, Taylor Hill is really just a west shoulder of Chicago Ridge. From Taylor Hill simply drop E into saddle 11,635. Then continue climbing E, sticking to the ridge, until you gain point 12,542 on Chicago Ridge. Ascend the ridge S from here ½ mile to the summit. The return is via the same route

SAFETY NOTES: Carefully judge slide hazard on the broad ridge leading to point 12,542 on Chicago Ridge. Watch for cornices on the ridge and don't let the excitement of a ski descent win over good judgment. With Colorado's midwinter snowpack, sticking to the ridges is how you survive years of mountaineering.

SUMMER: This is a fine alpine hike. It is not suitable for horses or bicycles.

Chapter 12 • 10th Mountain Division Hut

High on a gladed hillside near timber line, the 10th Mountain Division Hut is nestled in the arms of the Continental Divide. The log structure sleeps 16 and provides the standard 10th Mountain amenities, as well as a private upstairs bedroom.

ELEVATION: 11,370 feet
COUNTY: Lake
TEXT MAP: pp. 158-159
10TH MTN MAP: Galena Mountain
USGS MAP: Homestake Reservoir
TRAILHEADS: Tennessee Pass,
Crane Park

Completed during the summer of 1989, the hut was built with funds given by a group of 10th Mountain Division veterans: Bill Boddington (10th Mountain board), Col. Pete Peterson, Maury Kuper, and Bill Bowerman (see Appendix 2 for information about the 10th Mountain Division).

WARREN OHLRICH

For travel between the hut and the Tennessee Pass Trailhead, consider the 10th Mountain suggested route (12.1) that heads up the North Fork of West Tennessee Creek. While there are other possible routes, they have not been used enough for inclusion here. The route from the 10th Mountain Division Hut to Uncle Bud's Hut (12.3) dips through more than 6 main and subsidiary drainages as it parallels the Continental Divide. You'll get good use out of your map on this route!

Plenty of mellow ski terrain surrounds the 10th Mountain Division Hut.

You can make short scenic timber-line probes or enjoy glade skiing at lower elevations. For experts, the Continental Divide looms above with plenty of peak climbs, bowl skiing, and ridge runs. In particular, cone-shaped Homestake Peak just begs to be skied.

There are several befuddling aspects to ski touring in this area, mostly arising from trail marking. First of all, portions of the Main Range Trail shown on the USGS are not accurate. This is due to rerouting of the trail over the years. Secondly, the Main Range Trail is used for part of the Colorado Trail, which extends from Durango to Denver. As a result, the names Main Range Trail and Colorado Trail are often synonymous. The Colorado Trail is marked with small white triangles with the words Colorado Trail. Thirdly, there is a system of Forest Service managed ski trails (the Tennessee Pass ski touring trails) used as portions of the Colorado Trail, and in turn used as 10th Mountain trails. The problem is that these are marked with blue diamonds similar to 10th Mountain blue diamonds. Finally, there is a network of marked snowmobile trails (marked with orange diamonds). The 10th Mountain suggested routes both intersect and follow these trails, hence the possibility of confusion. Basically, the way you deal with this situation is by extra careful map, compass, and altimeter use. Wherever possible, the route descriptions below attempt to clarify points of confusion.

12.1

Tennessee Pass Trailhead — 10th Mountain Division Hut via North Fork West Tennessee Creek

DIFFICULTY: Intermediate
TIME: 5 hours up, 3 ½ hours down
DISTANCE: 5 ¾ miles
ELEVATION GAIN: 1,150 feet; elevation loss: 204 feet
10TH MTN MAP: Galena Mountain
USGS MAPS: Leadville North, Homestake Reservoir

This 10th Mountain suggested route avoids several popular snowmobile trails, but still uses some "sled" play areas. It's primary purpose is to connect 10th Mountain Division Hut with Vance's Cabin as described in route 11.4. For the most efficient access to the 10th Mountain Division Hut, use the Crane Park Trailhead route (12.2).

ROUTE DESCRIPTION: Start at the Tennessee Pass Trailhead parking lot with cross country wax. At the south edge of the lot, about 100 feet from Highway 24, you'll find a Forest Service "double post" trailhead sign. One trail leads SW and soon branches into the trails of the Forest Service

WHITE RIVER NATIONAL FOREST

HOLY CROSS WILDERNESS

continued on pp. 138-139

10th Mountain Hut & Trail System

The 10th Mountain Trail is located in the White River and San Isabel National Forests under agreement with the Forest Service, USDA.

Trails are marked by blue diamonds, except in wilderness areas where trails are marked by tree blazes.

This map is not a substitute for good route finding skills, it is just an aid to help locate routes.

Trails are not groomed and their exact location may vary.

© 1989 - 10th Mountain Trail Association

SCALE IN MILES

Hut
Trailhead

Tennessee Pass Trailhead
10,424'

Crane Park Trailhead
10,437'

1.30 miles to Crane Park
2.64 miles to Tennessee Pass
3.07 miles to 10th Mountain Division Hut
7.00 miles to Uncle Bud's Hut

2.74 miles to 10th Mountain Division Hut
2.97 miles to Tennessee Pass
6.67 miles to Uncle Bud's Hut

This map includes U.S. Forest Service as trails that correspond with the 10th Mountain Trail in several locations.

1.72 miles to 10th Mountain Division Hut
3.99 miles to Tennessee Pass

1.46 miles to 10th Mountain Division Hut
5.79 miles to Uncle Bud's Hut

2.76 miles to 10th Mountain Division Hut
4.50 miles to Uncle Bud's Hut
5.29 miles to Tennessee Pass

3.03 miles to Uncle Bud's Hut
4.22 miles to 10th Mountain Division Hut

10th Mountain Division Hut
11,370'

11.2
11.4
12.4

11.4
12.1
12.4

12.2

11.4
12.1
12.2
12.4

12.5

12.3
13.3

12.6

12.7

158

SAN ISABEL NATIONAL FOREST

Tennessee Park

Porcupine Gulch

Temple Gulch

Shingle Mill Gl.

St. Kevin Gulch

Griffin Tunnels

Road 107

1.82 miles to Uncle Bud's Hut
5.43 miles to 10th Mountain Division Hut

0.95 miles to Uncle Bud's Hut
4.30 miles to 10th Mountain Division Hut

Bud's Gulch

Uncle Bud's Hut

1.25 miles to Uncle Bud's Hut
4.30 miles to Turquoise Lake

13.4

Bear Lake

Galena Lake

13.5

13.5

St. Kevin Lake

Galena Mountain

4.3
13.2

Turquoise Lake Road

2.35 miles to Uncle Bud's Hut
3.20 miles to Turquoise Lake

13.1

1.40 miles to Turquoise Lake
4.15 miles to Uncle Bud's Hut

13.1

Parking Area

Boat Ramp

Turquoise Lake

TURQUOISE LAKE

Gravel Pit

Leadville Junction

Gravel Pit

Baby Doe Campground
May Brown Campground

Turquoise Lake Trailhead
9,880

Gaging Sta.

Sugarloaf Dam

Sugarloaf Gulch

Sugarloaf Mountain

Bartlett Gulch

Sugarloaf Gl. Gaging Sta.

Bald Eagle Mountain

Outlet

To Hagerman Pass

4.3
13.2

Busk Creek

159

managed Tennessee Pass ski touring area.

Take the trail starting at the "double post" trailhead, then stay left to follow the marked Colorado Trail (small white triangles). Basically, this section of the Colorado Trail parallels the Continental Divide by traversing several miles of hillside above Highway 24. At 2 ¼ miles the trail crosses through a small gulch at 10,380 feet, then climbs a short distance to cross the obvious Wurts Ditch Road at 10,480 feet. Look out for snowmobiles here!

Drop S then SW from the Wurts Ditch Road to intersect another road at 10,320 feet in the West Tennessee Creek drainage. Put your skins on here. Take care here not to drop onto a lower road into West Tennessee Creek. Instead, stay right and follow the road the leads up the North Fork of West Tennessee Creek 1 mile to Lily Lake (10,589 feet).

Swing right (N) at Lily Lake, cross the creek and a marshy area, then climb ½ mile N to a low-angled clearing. From here the route climbs NW 1 ¼ miles along the south side of the south fork of Slide Creek through a series of clearings, until it reaches the south end of a large flat marshy area just below and to the S of the hut. The trail to this point can be confusing because of myriad snowmobile and ski tracks. In general, it follows the south Slide Creek drainage, but winds around enough to make "drainage tracking" hard. You're best insurance is to take great care at Lily Lake to identify the distinct cone of Homestake Peak. Using this as a landmark, pay attention to your map, compass, and altimeter to stick to the trail. The route is marked by 10th Mountain, but don't depend on trail markers for navigation.

You can see the hut from the south side of the last low-angled marshy clearing — it's perched on a low-angled hillside on the north side of the clearing. With poor visibility this could be a confusing area, so take care.

REVERSE ROUTE DESCRIPTION: If you're skiing from hut to trailhead, you're in for a treat. First, ski the 10th Mountain suggested route across the flat clearing SW of the hut, then take the fall line and enjoy a ski run through clearings down to Lily Lake. At Lily Lake, intersect the North Fork Road and follow it down to a road fork at 10,340 feet. Turn left (N) off the road at the fork onto the Colorado Trail (also a marked 10th Mountain trail) and climb through a burn area, then through timber ⅓ mile NE and N to the obvious Wurts Ditch Road (10,480 feet). Cross the Wurts Ditch Road, drop into a small gulch, then ski a long 2 ¼-mile traverse E and NE through timber to the Tennessee Pass Trailhead.

SAFETY NOTES: This is a relatively mellow route. It does take some confusing permutations to avoid the snowmobile trails, so put energy into your navigation.

SUMMER: The roads and trails marked on the USGS maps make fine horse, bike, and hike routes for this hut. For regional routes, the Wurts Ditch Road is a fabulous bike ride in its own right, as is the Slide Lake jeep trail. Cyclists should be aware of the wilderness boundaries; they are marked on the text maps. The 10th Mountain trail that traverses from Tennessee Pass into the West Tennessee Creek drainage is only suitable for skiing.

12.2

Crane Park Trailhead — 10th Mountain Division Hut via West Tennessee Creek

DIFFICULTY: Intermediate
TIME: 4 ½ hours up, 3 hours down
DISTANCE: 4 ½ miles
ELEVATION GAIN: 1,353 feet; elevation loss: 120 feet
10TH MTN MAP: Galena Mountain
USGS MAPS: Leadville North, Homestake Reservoir

This route follows most of route 12.1, but has a more direct access from the Crane Park Trailhead. The actual Crane Park Trailhead varies with snow closure (see Chapter 1, Crane Park Trailhead).

ROUTE DESCRIPTION: To begin, either drive or ski up the gravel pit road from Crane Park to the obvious intersection of the Wurts Ditch Road. If you end up at the gravel pit, you have gone too far. The Wurts Ditch Road is usually well signed, but signs have a way of changing. Ski up the well-traveled, snow-covered Wurts Ditch Road just over ¼ mile to 10,480 feet. Here you turn left (S) off the road onto the Colorado Trail and follow route 12.1 to the hut.

REVERSE ROUTE DESCRIPTION: Follow route 12.1 to the Wurts Ditch Road. Turn right (SE) on the Wurts Ditch Road and follow it ¼ mile downhill to the aforementioned gravel pit road. This is the trailhead if the gravel pit road is plowed. If it is not plowed, turn left (N) and follow the gravel pit road to snow closure near Crane Park.

SAFETY NOTES: This route is very short, but stay alert and leave the trailhead before noon!

SUMMER: The 2 ¾-mile Slide Lake jeep trail from Wurts Ditch Road is a fine mountain bike route. See route 12.1 for other summer information.

12.3

10th Mountain Division Hut to Uncle Bud's Hut via Colorado Trail

DIFFICULTY: Intermediate
TIME: 8 hours
DISTANCE: 7 ¼ miles
ELEVATION GAIN: 1,460 feet; elevation loss: 1,450 feet
10TH MTN MAP: Galena Mountain
USGS MAP: Homestake Reservoir

For all practical purposes this 10th Mountain suggested route is the only intermediate trail from the 10th Mountain Division Hut to Uncle Bud's Hut. Lower routes would follow devious tracks through dark forest and force you to share trails with snowmobiles. Higher routes are all advanced and expert, mainly because of avalanche terrain. This route is longer than it looks on the map, and traverses through many subsidiary drainages. This is a change for skiers used to chugging up and down valleys, and requires attentive map work. The route is scenic, with changing views of the Mosquito Range to the E and the Continental Divide to the W and S. The various trails in this area can cause confusion (see the chapter introduction).

ROUTE DESCRIPTION: Start without skins, perhaps with a bit of cross country wax. From the front "window-wall" of the 10th Mountain Division Hut, ski S into the large marshy clearing, then S across the clearing to intersect a stream in a shallow gulch. The trail splits at this point, with the left (E) fork following routes 12.1/12.2 to trailheads. For your route, take the right (W) fork and follow the standard marked 10th Mountain trail as it traverses SW to a small pond, then drops through a clearing S to the North Fork West Tennessee Creek (11,100 feet), your second drainage crossing from the hut (count them as you go).

Continue S as you climb a small ridge (11,130 feet) that separates the North Fork West Tennessee Creek from the west fork of West Tennessee Creek. Next, drop S through timber to 10,980 feet in the beautiful open valley of West Tennessee Creek. Navigation in West Tennessee Creek can be difficult when visibility isn't the best. Cross the middle fork of West Tennessee Creek, then climb ¼ mile SW to a flat marshy area at West Tennessee Creek (11,080 feet).

Swing E for ¼ mile through the marshy area, then enter a trail cut through dark timber. Follow this trail E, then turn right (S) and climb to a small lake. From this lake climb to a small saddle (11,140 feet), then drop S through a clearing into a marshy area in a subsidiary drainage. Cross S through the marshy area and continue descending SE to intersect the Colorado Trail at 10,880 feet. (At this point the Colorado Trail is marked on the USGS map as the Main Range Trail. To add to the confusion, it is also the Longs Gulch Trail in the USFS Tennessee Pass ski touring trail system.)

Turn right and follow the trail as it leads SW 1 ¼ miles up Longs Gulch to 10,900 feet. Here you'll see some possible avalanche slopes on the north side of the drainage. Avoid these by staying in the timber to the S of the trail. Regain the trail in the timber and follow it as it climbs SW to a flat saddle with several small lakes. This saddle at 11,480 feet separates Porcupine Gulch and Longs Gulch.

Drop S into Porcupine Gulch from the saddle and cross Porcupine Creek at 11,240 feet. Still counting drainages? Climb S out of Porcupine Gulch, pass timber line, and continue climbing to 11,800 feet on an alpine shoulder. This is the high point of your route. The climb out of Porcupine Gulch switchbacks up through a slice of timber to avoid avalanche slopes to the right (W), then stays high to pass above other avalanche prone slopes. Take extra care to choose a safe route here, as you could easily deviate into avalanche terrain. The trail as marked on the text map is accurate, while the trail on the USGS map is inaccurate. If you have time, take a scenic detour at the shoulder and climb point 12,313.

At any rate, it's mostly downhill from the shoulder to Uncle Bud's Hut, so strip your skins. From your position on the shoulder, ski E down to to timber line at a sparsely timbered saddle (11,680 feet). At this point it is very important to swing W and stay in Bud's Gulch (unnamed on the USGS map, marked on the text map), since it's all to easy to ski the tempting glades down into St. Kevin Creek and end up far from the hut. A compass check can help you here.

Skiing down Bud's Gulch takes you through timber for 400 vertical feet to 11,360 feet, where you broach an elongated low-angled clearing. The 10th Mountain marked route follows the Colorado Trail down the left side of the clearing to 11,260 feet. You then swing E and climb through sparse timber ⅛ mile and 120 vertical feet back up to the hut.

This last little climb can be bothersome after all the drainages you've trudged through. On the map it looks like you can contour to the hut from the upper end of Bud's Gulch, but this route is blocked by some fairly dense forest. The alternate that works — if you are good with navigation — is to ski the wide rib dividing St. Kevin Gulch from Bud's Gulch. You may encounter a few snowmobiles here, but you'll get to the hut quicker. Stay to the east side of the rib in light timber and traverse the east side of several bumps. Again, don't drop down into St. Kevin Gulch. The hut is only visible from several hundred feet away on either route.

SAFETY NOTES: Refer to your map often on this route, as cutting all the drainages can be confusing. An altimeter can help a great deal with this sort of skiing. You drop into a drainage, read your elevation, and you know exactly where you are (provided you have counted drainages).

SUMMER: The Colorado Trail is a fine hike or horse route. Most of the route is within designated wilderness, so cyclists should look for other routes. Portions of the 10th Mountain route described above (those that leave the established trails) are marked ski trails with no summer tread.

12.4
10th Mountain Division Hut to Vance's Cabin via Tennessee Pass

DIFFICULTY: Intermediate
TIME: 8 hours
DISTANCE: 9 miles
ELEVATION GAIN: 760 feet; elevation loss: 1,150 feet
10TH MTN MAPS: Galena Mountain and Chicago Ridge
USGS MAPS: Homestake Reservoir, Leadville North, Pando

This 10th Mountain suggested route is the standard ski-through between the 10th Mountain Division Hut and Vance's Cabin. It crosses a major highway at Tennessee Pass, then passes by the Ski Cooper. If you're on a long ski-through, plan a resupply for the highway.

ROUTE DESCRIPTION: From the 10th Mountain Division Hut, follow reverse route 12.1 to the parking area at Tennessee Pass. From there, take route 11.2 to Vance's Cabin.

SAFETY NOTES: See notes on routes 11.2 and 12.1.

SUMMER: See notes on routes 11.2 and 12.1.

12.5
Slide Lake from 10th Mountain Division Hut

DIFFICULTY: Intermediate
TIME: Several hours round trip
DISTANCE: 1 1/4 miles round trip
ELEVATION GAIN: 330 feet round trip
10TH MTN MAP: Galena Mountain
USGS MAP: Homestake Reservoir

If you itch for a timber-line tour but lack the skills to climb the divide or ski the couloirs, take a scenic cruise to Slide Lake.

ROUTE DESCRIPTION: The route is simple. Put your skins on at the hut, then simply climb the hill NW of the hut, bearing right (N) as the hill gets steeper. At timber line, around 11,500 feet, keep Homestake Peak on your front left as you continue to Slide Lake (11,700 feet) in a superb high basin. On the return, ski the glades that tempted you as you climbed.

SAFETY NOTES: Avoid avalanche slopes on all sides of the Homestake Peak basin.

SUMMER: This is a fine horse ride or hike. Cyclists can ride the Slide Lake jeep trail to the marked wilderness boundary just below the lake.

12.6

Homestake Peak from 10th Mountain Division Hut

DIFFICULTY: Advanced
TIME: 5 hours round trip
DISTANCE: 4 1/2 miles round trip
ELEVATION GAIN: 1,839 feet round trip
10TH MTN MAP: Galena Mountain
USGS MAP: Homestake Reservoir

In Colorado, about 736 peaks top the 13,000-foot mark. One of these is Homestake Peak (13,209 feet), W of the 10th Mountain Division Hut. A classic glacier-made cone, Homestake has a relatively avalanche safe climbing route, and makes a good branch route from the hut. Most of the ski lines are too avalanche prone for safe winter descents, but the ascent route (east ridge) can yield some fine lines, provided the snow has not been wind-scoured. Consider a trip to Homestake Peak during the spring corn snow season.

ROUTE DESCRIPTION: To climb Homestake Peak, follow route 12.5 to Slide Lake. From the south side of the lake, climb SE about 1/4 mile and 200 vertical feet to a vegetated hillock at the 11,900-foot level. From here avoid the avalanche runouts from Homestake's east ridge by contouring and gently climbing low-angled terrain to the broad ridge crest. Simply follow the ridge to the summit. The ascent route is the safest descent. During the spring corn season you can enjoy some great ski lines down the north face of the east ridge from about the 12,400-foot level. For a real corn fest, ski the bowls from the Continental Divide S of the peak, then traverse back to the hut. You'll find other corn snow lines around Slide Lake.

SAFETY NOTES: While ascending the east ridge, evaluate avalanche dangers to either side. Don't let temptation lead you into skiing down dangerous slopes.

SUMMER: This is a fine summit hike that adds a "thirteener" to your list.

12.7
Continental Divide Ridge from 10th Mountain Division Hut

DIFFICULTY: Expert
TIME: Full day round trip
DISTANCE: At least 5 miles round trip
ELEVATION GAIN: 2,000 feet round trip
10TH MTN MAP: Galena Mountain
USGS MAP: Homestake Reservoir

One of the safest ways for advanced mountaineers to enjoy the winter high country is by doing ridge runs. The Continental Divide S from Homestake Peak is a fine candidate for such an endeavor. At the least, you can make a short probe to several small bumps close to the summit of Homestake, enjoy the view, then get back to the hut by tea time. At the most, you can take the Divide to Galena Mountain, then descend to Turquoise Lake or Uncle Bud's Hut.

ROUTE DESCRIPTION: To do this route, take route 12.6 to the summit of Homestake Peak, then simply stick to the Divide ridge as it leads S. Where logic dictates, make small traverses below the high points of the ridge, usually on the west side.

SAFETY NOTES: You're very exposed to storms on a ridge such as this. In midwinter, most escape routes will be cut off by avalanche danger. Thus, you must plan this ridge run with care. Also, if you plan on traversing the entire ridge, a good weather prediction is mandatory (see Appendix 4). Consider corn snow season for this route, as avalanche danger will be more predictable and the weather will be milder.

SUMMER: This is a fine hike. Beware of afternoon lightning.

Chapter 13 • Uncle Bud's Hut

Uncle Bud's Hut, owned by 10th Mountain, is similar in aspect and construction to the 10th Mountain Division Hut. Views from the south window-wall include a panorama of 14,421-foot Mount Massive and the logged

ELEVATION:	11,380 feet
COUNTY:	Lake
TEXT MAP:	pp. 158-159
10TH MTN MAP:	Galena Mountain
USGS MAP:	Homestake Reservoir
TRAILHEADS:	Turquoise Lake, Elk Wallow Campground

pate of Bald Eagle Mountain. During the mining boom in the late 1800s, the land around Leadville was logged off like Bald Eagle. That there are any forests at all is a testament to the hearty species of conifer that grace the Rockies.

The hut was built as a memorial to 10th Mountain Division veteran Bud Winter, who died in Italy during World War II. He was a "born skier and mountaineer" and dearly remembered. Funds for the hut were given by Bud's brother, Dr. Fred Winter. His sister Laura contributed the proceeds from her poetry book *Laura's Lines*.

WARREN OHLRICH

This hut allows skiers to travel over Hagerman Pass to the Fryingpan drainage (route 13.2), thus forming a huge loop that strong skiers can enjoy. 10th Mountain suggested routes, however, are intended for intermediate skiers, so several more huts are planned to shorten the route to the Fryingpan. For ski-throughs to the north, routes 13.3 and 13.4 use sections of the Colorado Trail (marked on the USGS maps as the Main Range Trail) for a complex route that parallels the Continental Divide. This trail cuts across more than 6 main and subsidiary drainages—it's scenic, complex, and fun.

Uncle Bud's Hut is very accessible from Leadville via a short trailhead to hut route from Turquoise Lake (route 13.1). Using this trail, experts can get to the hut quickly, then spend a few days base skiing. Freshman skiers can use this route as a step on the learning ladder. Branch routes from the hut range from mellow glade skiing to skiing euro-style couloirs on Galena Mountain.

13.1

Turquoise Lake Trailhead—Uncle Bud's Hut

DIFFICULTY: Intermediate
TIME: 6 hours up, 4 hours down
DISTANCE: 5 ½ miles
ELEVATION GAIN: 1,520 feet; elevation loss: 20 feet
10TH MTN MAP: Galena Mountain
USGS MAPS: Leadville North, Homestake Reservoir

This 10th Mountain suggested route follows snow-covered roads through a beautiful lodgepole pine forest. It is a short route, with relatively easy navigation.

ROUTE DESCRIPTION: Begin with cross country wax at the Turquoise Lake Trailhead. Ski, drive, or walk (depending on snow cover) N then W on the main road. This road gradually climbs, while paralleling the north shore of the lake. It is very distinct and easy to follow, the only possible false turns being several well-signed spurs to boat ramps and campgrounds. At 3.2 miles (10,410 feet) leave the main road by turning right (N) onto a well-defined road cut. There is a stake here with the road number 107, but this may be covered by snow. There are also the standard 10th Mountain trail markers. All the following mileages are measured from this turn.

Put your skins on and follow road 107 as it climbs N through conifer. If you notice, just ¼ mile after turning from the main road, you'll pass an intersection at 10,570 feet. Be sure to stay N on 107 here. It can be all to easy, especially on an overcast day, to loose your bearings. Use your compass and altimeter.

At ½ mile from the main road, you'll pass under a power line at 10,730 feet. This is a good landmark and altimeter calibration point. After the power line, the road climbs N a short distance, swings W for about ⅓ mile, then makes a short steep climb N several hundred feet to a mining area in some flats (11,000 feet). Stay on the road in this area, as there are several open shafts that can be hidden by snow. Though most mine evidence will be obscured by snow, you'll see lots of unnatural looking mounds and some wood ruins.

Ski road 107 W through the mining area, then begin a climb NW ½ mile (still on the road) to a clearing at 11,280 feet. The road to this point follows the ridge between St. Kevin Creek and Turquoise Lake, so as long as you're climbing you're on the route.

At the 11,280-foot clearing the 10th Mountain suggested route leaves road 107 and takes a climbing traverse another ¼ mile NW to Uncle Bud's Hut (11,380 feet) at the top end of the clearing. The hut is visible from several hundred yards below. The possible mistake here would be to stay on 107 and traverse below the hut. You can see the hut from 107, so keep looking uphill for it. Also, use your altimeter as you get close.

REVERSE ROUTE DESCRIPTION: Descending road 107 can be slightly hairy, as there are some tree-lined "toboggan chutes". From the front of Uncle Bud's Hut, take a descending traverse SE through a clearing. Intersect road 107 at 11,280 feet. Stay on the road as it takes you downhill along the crest of the ridge between St. Kevin Gulch and Turquoise Lake. Swing N then SE through a flat area at the 11,000-foot level, then climb a small hill to a mining area.

Take care to find the road cut at the east end of the mining area, where it makes a right turn (S) down a steep hill. From here the road cut is easy to follow down to the main Turquoise Lake road. Turn left (E) on the Turquoise Lake road and follow it 3.2 miles to the Turquoise Lake Trailhead (or to a closer snow closure).

SAFETY NOTES: This short route could lull you into false security. The problem is that many snowmobiles and backcountry skiers use the area, so there could be trails leading everywhere.

SUMMER: Road 107 is a fine horse, hike, or bike route. Cyclists should note the wilderness boundary just W of Uncle Bud's Hut.

13.2

Fryingpan Drainage — Uncle Bud's Hut via Hagerman Pass

DIFFICULTY: Advanced
TIME: Very long day or overnight camp
DISTANCE: 21 miles
ELEVATION GAIN: 4,881 feet; elevation loss: 2,328 feet (from Elk Wallow
  Campground Trailhead)
10TH MTN MAP: Galena Mountain and Mount Yeckel
USGS MAPS: Homestake Reservoir, Mt. Massive, Nast, Meredith

This alternate trail connects the Leadville 10th Mountain huts with the
Fryingpan drainage (Diamond J Guest Ranch and Rocky Mountain
Health Ranch). It is the only route in this book that takes a high pass and
thus will attract "alpine" wilderness skiers. Future plans call for several
more huts near this route. At this time the trail is long and arduous.

ROUTE DESCRIPTION:

From the Elk Wallow Campground Trailhead ski S ¼ mile across the bottom land to the point where the obvious power lines start up the mountain
side. Put your skins on here and ski up the well-defined road cut that
begins a few feet S of the power lines. After about a mile of snow-covered
road, you will reach Diemer Lake.

At the north end of Diemer Lake, ski W up an obvious road cut that climbs
around the lake basin to a 10,031-foot saddle N of the lake. From the saddle, ski the road SW ¾ mile to the main Hagerman Pass road at Sellar
Park. Experts can drop directly south about 280 vertical feet to the road
(dense timber). Next, enjoy a long trudge up the road all the way to Hagerman Pass. This road follows the old Colorado Midland Railroad grade. At
10,690 feet the road takes a long climbing traverse to the pass. This section
is usually wind-scoured, but could pose some avalanche risk. To avoid the
traverse, ski up the valley to the east end of Ivanhoe Lake, then climb a
more direct route to the pass. Even this route can be risky, so beware.

From Hagerman Pass (still on the road), take a dropping traverse E to timber line. As this traverse can have some slide danger, consider leaving the
road at the pass, traversing to the ridge that descends N from point 12,085,
then descending this ridge to intersect the road at timber line. From timber
line, continue 1 ½ miles NE and E through patchy timber to an important
right (S) turn at 11,300 feet. The road then traverses SW down the side of
the Busk Creek drainage, crosses Busk Creek (10,760 feet), then follows
the Busk Creek valley down to 10,360 feet. Leave the main road here and
descend the the Main Range Trail (Colorado Trail) to the Turquoise Lake
road. Ski the Turquoise Lake road around the west end of the lake, then 2

miles along the north side of the lake (the road is some distance above the lake) to a creek that drops from the vicinity of Uncle Bud's Hut. If you're a good map reader, you can spot this creek and use it as a route to Uncle Bud's Hut. If you can't find the creek, continue on the Turquoise Lake road for 1 1/4 mile to the intersection of road 107, where you then follow route 13.1 to Uncle Bud's Hut.

REVERSE ROUTE DESCRIPTION: From Uncle Bud's Hut, the first step for this route is to get down to the Turquoise Lake road from the hut. This can be done via route 13.1, but that puts you several miles farther E than you'd be if you drop directly down the drainage S of the hut.

Ski the snow-covered Turquoise Lake road W to the west end of Turquoise Lake and continue on the road as it climbs S then E to cross Busk Creek at 9,960 feet. A few hundred yards E of Busk Creek, leave the road and climb the Colorado Trail 400 vertical feet to the Hagerman Pass road. Turn right (W) and follow the Hagerman Pass road as it climbs 3 miles up the southeast side of the Busk Creek drainage, crossing Busk Creek at 10,796 feet. After this crossing, the road steepens and climbs the northwest side of the Busk Creek drainage to 11,300 feet.

At 11,300 feet the road swings SW then W, winding through patchy timber to timber line. Above timber line the road traverses north-facing slopes to Hagerman Pass (11,925 feet). To avoid slide danger on these traverses, consider leaving the road at timber line and climbing the ridge S of the road. At the pass, if the snow is skiable, leave the road and enjoy a run down to Ivanhoe Lake. If you must walk the wind-striped tundra, it is probably best to use the road that traverses downhill NW from the pass. In either case, follow the road down Ivanhoe Creek, then up through Hell Gate where the road traverses the side of a ridge. After Hell Gate follow the road to 9,648 feet in Sellar Park. Leave the main road here and turn N onto a subsidiary road that climbs 3/4 mile through timber to a saddle (10,031 feet). Take the road NE from the saddle as it drops NE then W to Diemer Lake, then continues N to the Elk Wallow Campground Trailhead.

SAFETY NOTES: Don't be a sheep and thoughtlessly follow roads. If judgment dictates, leave the road to avoid avalanche slopes or to travel a more efficient line. There can be avalanche danger where the road traverses the side of Busk Creek valley. You can avoid this traverse by using the railroad grade several hundred vertical feet above.

SUMMER: All the roads in this area are fine bicycle routes. Hikers and equestrians should stick to the trails, as the roads have a great deal of auto traffic. Cycling from the Fryingpan to Leadville is popular. While you can cycle the route from Elk Wallow Campground, a more efficient route uses the main Fryingpan Road.

13.3

Uncle Bud's Hut to 10th Mountain Division Hut via Colorado Trail

DIFFICULTY: Intermediate
TIME: 8 hours up
DISTANCE: 7 1/4 miles
ELEVATION GAIN: 1,450 feet; elevation loss: 1,460 feet
10TH MTN MAP: Galena Mountain
USGS MAP: Homestake Reservoir

This 10th Mountain suggested route is the only practical intermediate route between Uncle Bud's Hut and the 10th Mountain Division Hut. The route is long and, unlike most "valley" 10th Mountain routes, cuts through many drainages. You'll find plenty of good views on this trail. The 14,000-foot peaks of the Mosquito Range loom to the E and the majestic Continental Divide rises to the W and S. As you can see on the USGS map, this route uses sections of the Colorado Trail (marked on the map as the Main Range Trail). The 10th Mountain route deviates in places from this trail for more efficient ski lines and to avoid avalanche slopes.

ROUTE DESCRIPTION: To begin, leave your skins off and glide W from the hut for several hundred yards down into an elongated clearing (Bud's Gulch). At the bottom of the hill put your skins on at the wilderness boundary sign, ski N up the east side of the clearing, then enter the trees at the north end of the clearing (11,360 feet). Continue climbing NE to a sparsely timbered saddle at 11,680 feet. From the saddle climb W 1/4 mile up the ridge to 11,800 feet. This is the high point of the route and a good place for a long session with map and compass. Remember that these wilderness trails are marked with tree blazes.

Strip your skins on the ridge, then take a dropping traverse NW into Porcupine Gulch. To avoid avalanche terrain, this traverse starts above the marked route of the Colorado Trail, then drops down short switchbacks through a strip of timber into Porcupine Gulch. Sticking to this timber avoids avalanche terrain to either side. Experts may wish to ski a good run W of the timber, but use careful slide safety procedures with this option. Cross Porcupine Creek at 11,240 feet. Next, climb up the north side of Porcupine Creek to a broad, flat saddle at 11,480 feet (with several small lakes). This short climb is hardly worth reskinning for; try a bit of cross country wax under the middle of your ski, or just herringbone.

From the broad saddle, drop N via two switchbacks into Longs Gulch. Cross Longs Creek at 10,900 feet and leave the Holy Cross Wilderness 400 feet E of the creek crossing. Next follow the Colorado Trail down through intermittent clearings on the north side of Longs Creek to 10,740 feet. At this point your route (still on the Colorado Trail) climbs NE out of Longs Gulch, then around the shoulder that separates Longs Gulch from the West Tennessee Creek drainages. The Colorado Trail continues E here but your route travels N, so leave the Colorado Trail when it starts to drop E (10,880 feet) and take a climbing traverse N to cross the south fork of West Tennessee Creek at 10,990 feet.

Climb up another shoulder N out of the south fork of West Tennessee Creek, then descend N past a small lake (11,140 feet). After the lake, continue N a few hundred yards, then traverse W through dark timber and across a marshy clearing. Swing NE and drop ¼ mile into the clearings of the main West Tennessee Creek drainage. From 10,980 feet in West Tennessee Creek, climb NE then N over a small shoulder into the North Fork of West Tennessee Creek (11,100 feet), then N onto a sparsely treed hillside. Climb the west side of this clear area to a small lake at 11,340 feet.

You will now be in another relatively flat area. From the east side of the lake, ski E several hundred yards through timber, then swing NE and ski through ¼ mile of intermittent clearings to a large flat clearing just S of the hut. You can see the hut from here; the trail crosses the clearing.

SAFETY NOTES: On the 10th Mountain suggested route above, there is no place where you will be exposed to avalanches. Slight deviations from this route, however, will expose you to slide danger. There are many avalanche slopes up above timber line. As you can see from the above description, this is a complex route. Allow plenty of time for orienteering.

SUMMER: The Colorado Trail is a fine hike or horse ride. Most of the trail is in designated wilderness, where possession of a bicycle is a crime. The sections of the 10th Mountain route that deviate from the Colorado Trail have no summer tread.

13.4

Galena Lake from Uncle Bud's Hut

DIFFICULTY: Intermediate
TIME: 3 hours round trip
DISTANCE: 2 ½ miles round trip
ELEVATION GAIN: 310 feet round trip
10TH MTN MAP: Galena Mountain
USGS MAP: Homestake Reservoir

This short branch route takes the Colorado Trail to Galena Lake, but you could certainly continue exploring past the lake.

ROUTE DESCRIPTION: From Uncle Bud's Hut, ski W down into the clearing in the drainage W of the hut (Bud's Gulch). Do not ski up Bud's Gulch, simply cross to the west side of the clearing and locate the obvious Forest Service "double post" trailhead sign (11,240 feet); this marks the Main Range Trail (the route of the Colorado Trail).

Ski W out of Bud's Gulch on the Colorado Trail. It takes a short climb up through timber, then traverses ¼ mile to the top of a clearing at 11,240 feet. The Colorado Trail takes a dropping traverse from here, then passes between north and south Galena Lakes. For a better ski route, take the fall line down to the flat marshy area where the clearing widens, then ski fairly flat terrain SW a short distance to Galena Lake. Take some time to explore the area; include Bear Lake in your quest. Return via the same route.

SAFETY NOTES: This is a very mellow excursion, with no real safety problems. Remember that the Main Range Trail (Colorado Trail) is marked with tree blazes and the occasional small white triangles. Pay attention to your map, since it's likely you will deviate from the summer trail.

SUMMER: This is a fine horse ride or hike. No bicycles are allowed.

13.5

Galena Mountain from Uncle Bud's Hut

DIFFICULTY: Advanced to Expert
TIME: Full day
DISTANCE: 4 ½ miles round trip
ELEVATION GAIN: 2,900 feet round trip
10TH MTN MAP: Galena Mountain
USGS MAP: Homestake Reservoir

Rising to the W of Uncle Bud's Hut, Galena Mountain (12,893 feet) is sure to tempt mountaineers. While lower than the 13,000-foot and 14,000-foot peaks that stud the Continental Divide in the Leadville area, Galena Mountain offers good variety and it is very accessible from the hut.

ROUTE DESCRIPTION: For a winter ascent, there are two feasible routes. The shorter option, rated expert, ascends the prominent east ridge from 11,680 feet on the Colorado Trail. The first part of the east ridge is a simple ridge run. After a deep notch (12,600 feet), rope work is necessary to climb a vertical step. In the winter you must ascend this step to avoid avalanche danger on the northeast face. But in the spring, provided the snow is frozen spring corn, you can avoid the technical climbing by traversing onto the northeast face. This option requires expert snow climbing skills.

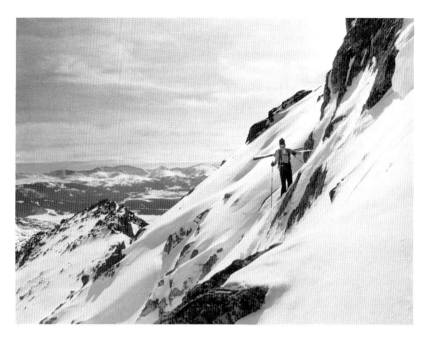

Traversing into the north face of Galena Mountain to avoid the rock climbing on the east ridge.

The longer winter route, rated advanced, leaves from the Colorado Trail at the small lake just W of Galena Lake (see route 13.4). From the small lake, you take a short climbing traverse W up onto the broad south ridge of Galena Mountain. You follow this ridge to the summit, either sticking to the right hand (E) ridge crest, or following the broad ridge. Your choice would be dictated by avalanche conditions.

This route also makes a good descent from the peak.

Finally, expert mountaineers will enjoy the beautiful couloir that ascends to the summit of Galena Mountain from St. Kevin Lake. At 48 degrees maximum angle, this couloir makes both a good crampon climb or "extreme ski" during the spring season on a frozen spring snowpack. The most straightforward route to St. Kevin Lake follows the Bear Lake drainage from the Colorado Trail.

SAFETY NOTES: All these routes pass through avalanche terrain and thus are safer on a spring "melt-freeze" snowpack while the snow is frozen in the morning.

SUMMER: The east ridge of Galena Mountain is a fine summer climb and the south ridge makes a good alpine hike.

Appendix 1 • **Hut Data**

Hut	Built	Elevation	County	USGS map
McNamara Hut	1982	10,360	Pitkin	Thimble Rock
Margy's Hut	1982	11,300	Pitkin	Meredith
Diamond J Guest Ranch	1927	8,250	Pitkin	Meredith
Rocky Mt. Health Ranch	1965	8,760	Pitkin	Nast
Harry Gates Hut	1986	9,700	Eagle	Crooked Creek Pass
Peter Estin Hut	1985	11,200	Eagle	Crooked Creek Pass
Polar Star Inn	1987	11,040	Eagle	Fulford
Shrine Mountain Inn	1988	11,209	Summit	Vail Pass
Fowler/Hilliard Hut	1988	11,500	Eagle	Pando
Schuss/Zesiger Hut	1988	11,660	Eagle	Pando
Vance's Cabin	1988	10,980	Eagle	Pando
10th Mt. Division Hut	1989	11,370	Lake	Homestake Reservoir
Uncle Bud's Hut	1989	11,380	Lake	Homestake Reservoir

Appendix 2 • **A History of Camp Hale & the 10th Mountain Division**

The 10th Mountain Trail Association's name honors the soldiers of the 10th Mountain Division of the U.S. Army. The story of the '10th' is one of war, tragedy, excellence, and pride.

Fifty years ago, with the world at the brink of World War II, the U.S. War Department pondered the need for mountain troops. As an experiment, winter training was mandated for picked men from various divisions. The infant ski corps trained at Mount Rainier and made several trips into the Olympic Mountains. As a result, the army decided that training mountain troops was possible and they began a search for a training camp site.

The top location, West Yellowstone, Montana, was ruled out because of nearby trumpeter swans. Aspen was considered, but there was not enough space for 15,000 men!

Finally, a site was chosen in the Eagle River valley in the Colorado Rockies, just to the north of Tennessee Pass. It was named Camp Hale, after General Irving Hale from Denver.

To build the place, the army sent in thousands of construction workers. The 'Pando Constructors' graded three miles of the valley as flat as a golf course and rechanneled the river into a straight ditch. With the nearby mountains, cliffs, and rivers, it was an ideal spot to train mountain troops. Hale was completed November 16, 1942, and more than 11,000 troops moved in three weeks later. You'll see the flats of the Camp Hale site when you use the Pando, Camp Hale, and South Camp Hale trailheads.

The flats of the Camp Hale site.

Before Camp Hale was built and occupied, the army was skeptical about the need for mountain troops. But reality reared its head. In the Balkins, the invading Italians had been driven into the mountains by the Greeks. Winter hit. In addition to 25,000 battle deaths, more than 10,000 Italians died of exposure. It was a disaster and the U.S. Army took notice. As a result, the 87th Mountain Regiment was created on November 15, 1941.

The 87th was to train at Fort Lewis, Washington. It was hard to find men for the new group. In one novel move, the National Ski Patrol was actually made into an official army recruiter! Right off, the recruiting gave the impression that this was no ordinary group of soldiers. For example, three reference letters were required. Moreover, many famous skiers and climbers signed up. As a result, many ivyleaguers and non-army types joined out of a mistaken notion that it would be easy — or at least elite — duty.

After plenty of training, the 87th left Fort Lewis for their first campaign — the ironic invasion of Kiska, in the Aleutian Islands. A chapter of World War II that many have tried to forget, Kiska came about because the Japanese decided on a strategic occupation of these windlashed, arctic hunks of real estate. The U.S. could not abide such an affront. Things heated up when the 7th Infantry took Attu Island from the Japanese, but the island almost took them in the process. More than 12,000 men succumbed to trenchfoot alone. It was clear that men trained for the cold and wet were needed, so the 87th Mountain Regiment was selected as the invasion force for the second Japanese occupied island: Kiska.

A huge operation ensued. The troops had yet to see real battle, but they were primed. Transported by more than 100 ships, they were equipped with latest wet and cold weather gear. Under the cover of morning darkness they made a beach landing. Soon, their first fighting: the battalion headquarters was under attack. More gunfire; then nightfall. The next day, the men realized that they had been fighting each other. Finally, after days of fear and misery, it was discovered that the Japanese had left before the invasion!

With few losses, considering the confusion and weather of Kiska, the 87th returned to Fort Lewis. Then on December 6, 1942, the 87th moved lock-stock-and-barrel to Camp Hale. Life at the camp was appalling. Hundreds of lowlanders were tormented by the altitude. A pall of smog hung over the valley, causing a chronic cough known as the Pando Hack (after nearby Pando). In winter, the temperature hovered below zero for days, while strenuous drills never stopped. In the spring, the camp was was a sea of mud. To many of the soldiers, it was know as "Camp Hell".

The training was never ending, but out of Camp Hale came one of the most competent divisions in modern warfare. In fact, a German general said that the 10th was the finest division he had ever faced. Aside from days of rock climbing, alpine travel, and weapons practice, the winter training was what really set the mountain troops apart. In the two years at Camp Hale, two major maneuvers were carried out on Homestake Peak near the present site of the 10th Mountain Division Hut. The first was a disaster; many soldiers deliberately froze their feet to get out of the hills. But the next winter, the men redeemed themselves in an exemplary action on Homestake's slopes.

All was not roses however, as morale continued at a low ebb. Camp Hale was still a miserable place. The men got little pride from not being a division of their own. Also, there were chronic rumors that they would never see battle. The last straw was when, on June 22, 1944, the men were moved from Camp Hale to Camp Swift, Texas, to take part in maneuvers. Suddenly they were learning how to handle 4,000 mules, and rappelling off buildings. Something had to give, and it did.

General George Hays, a true military leader, was given command of the men. Morale was still low when Hays took charge. But by intensely training the men as a group, he made them into a tough fighting force with plenty of pride. Finally, on November 7, 1944, the outfit was officially named the 10th Mountain Division.

By January the 10th was in Italy. Here, they had a pivotal role in gaining the high ground in several battles. They scaled vertical cliffs to take Campiano Peak via Riva Ridge, then moved on to engage the Germans in the Battle of Mount Belvedere. This was the big one; the 10th had the summit in 24 hours. They went on to participate in the Po River offensive and were the first of the allied forces to reach and cross the Po. Losses were heavy; 990 soldiers gave their lives while fighting in Italy and Kiska. In the end, the 10th had gained a reputation as one of the toughest and most competent groups of soldiers to fight in World War II.

Hardship aside – or perhaps because of it – the men of the 10th developed a strong camaraderie, and many of them gained a great love for Colorado as well. After the war, hundreds of 10th veterans returned to Colorado to settle down. With their ski skills, knowledge of the land, and enthusiasm, many of these men were key figures in the development of Colorado's ski industry.

One such veteran, Fritz Benedict, settled in Aspen. He came with a dream of a winter trail network and realized his dream by spearheading the creation of the 10th Mountain Trail Association. Other 10th Mountain Division veterans have been involved with the 10th Mountain Trail Association as well. The late Jose Acebo served on the board of directors for 7 years, and a group of vets contributed the funds for the 10th Mountain Division Hut. For skiers on the 10th Mountain Trail, the 10th's most striking legacy is the Camp Hale site. After the solders left for Camp Swift, Camp Hale was used as a prisoner of war camp, then mostly razed. The 10th Mountain Division was deactivated in 1945. In 1985, a new 10th Mountain Division was organized at Camp Drum, New York. You'll find a memorial at the Camp Hale Trailhead, and a 10th veterans memorial at the summit of Tennessee Pass.

Appendix 3 • Equipment Check List

An old proverb says, "The heaviest baggage for a traveler is an empty purse". Though you don't need money in the wilds, you certainly need the proper gear in your pack. This check list will help you to that end. It might not include everything you would take, but it has the essentials. For details on things such as your first-aid kit, see the gear section in the primer.

Above all, remember that although using the huts allows you to carry a light pack, you should still carry the essentials for a night out: one gas stove per party, shovels, food, sleeping bags for each person, and some sort of bivouac shelter. Also, the best gear in the world will not help you unless it fits, functions, and you know how to use it. Plan your trips carefully, and be sure you have the necessary mountaineering skills for the trip you choose.

PERSONAL GEAR
- Insulating cap, such as a wool or pile ski cap
- Scarf or neck gaiter
- Mittens for extreme cold
- Ski gloves

- Leg gaiters (high top)
- Long underwear top and bottom
- Pile jacket
- Light layer such as pile vest
- Ski Pants or tights (no cotton)
- Shell parka and pants
- Socks, including extra pair
- Ski boots
- Skis, ski poles
- Climbing skins
- Backpack
- Sleeping bag (light weight – about 20 degree rated)
- Pillow case (oversized for large pillows at the huts)
- Wide mouth water bottle (at least one liter)
- Pocket knife
- Fire starting kit (matches, lighter, starting fuel etc.)
- Headlamp
- Goggles and sun glasses
- Sunscreen lotion and lip balm
- Shovel
- Avalanche rescue beacon (optional, depends on route)

GROUP GEAR

- Ski wax selection
- Stove
- First-aid kit
- Repair kit
- Bivouac shelter
- Maps, compass, altimeter, guidebook
- Thermometer
- Food (be sure plenty is edible without cooking, and that each person carries their own selection of trail food)

Appendix 4 • Weather Forecasting

RULES-OF-THUMB FOR FORECASTING WEATHER ON THE 10TH MOUNTAIN TRAILS

1. Steadily falling barometric pressure usually indicates a nearing storm. You can evaluate this and number 2 with your altimeter.

2. Steadily rising barometric pressure usually indicates clearing weather.

3. When barometric pressure is more than 30.10, rain or snow will probably end soon.

4. When the temperature during a storm drops to less than 5 degrees F,

snowfall will rapidly diminish.

5. Cirrus clouds can precede a storm by 24 hours or more. A ring around the moon is caused by thin cirrus.

6. Thickening and lowering clouds (usually coming from the west) indicate a nearing storm.

7. Thickening mountain wave clouds indicate increasing moisture and increasing winds aloft, and a possible nearing storm.

8. Mountain wave clouds and snow plumes on ridges, indicate high winds at mountaintop levels.

9. Thinning and lifting clouds indicate clearing weather.

10. Frontal passage (the end of a storm) is often indicated by the lowest point of the barometric pressure curve (you can plot this from your altimeter), a wind shift, and a sudden appearance of heavily rimmed snow crystals or graupel.

11. Current weather reports on radio, especially NOAA Weather Radio on the VHF band, are your best sources for accurate forecasts while mountaineering.

FROM COMPUSERVE, A PUBLIC DOMAIN SOURCE

Appendix 5 • Sun & Moon Times

For each date, this table gives the approximate time and direction for sunrise, sunset, moonrise, and moonset. All times are in 24 hour format, and are for a level horizon (they'll be different for a valley floor). Direction is in the form of an azimuth, which is simply the degrees on your compass dial the rise or set will occur (from geographic north). Moon phase is the percentage of a full moon, i.e. the date with .99 moon phase is the full moon.

Latitude: N 39.00   Longitude: W 106.00

NOTE: TIMES IN MST UNTIL NOTED

Date	Sunrise (azm)	Sunset (azm)	Moonrise(azm)	Moonset(azm)	Phase
12 NOV 1989	6:44 (98.0)	16:53 (233.1)	16:13 (47)	6:07 (281)	0.99
15 NOV 1989	6:48 (99.1)	16:50 (232.0)	19:00 (40)	9:52 (292)	0.90
30 NOV 1989	7:04 (103.3)	16:43 (227.9)	9:22 (111)	18:30 (220)	0.05
12 DEC 1989	7:14 (105.1)	16:42 (226.0)	16:37 (39)	7:28 (292)	0.99
15 DEC 1989	7:16 (105.4)	16:43 (225.8)	20:11 (51)	10:01 (282)	0.87
31 DEC 1989	7:23 (105.1)	16:52 (226.1)	9:48 (93)	20:48 (241)	0.13
10 JAN 1990	7:23 (103.5)	17:01 (227.7)	16:35 (43)	7:09 (289)	0.99
15 JAN 1990	7:22 (102.4)	17:06 (228.8)	22:11 (78)	9:46 (257)	0.78

Date	Sunrise (azm)	Sunset (azm)	Moonrise(azm)	Moonset(azm)	Phase
31 JAN 1990	7:12 (97.4)	17:24 (233.9)	9:35 (63)	23:19 (272)	0.27
9 FEB 1990	7:03 (93.8)	17:35 (237.4)	17:47 (59)	6:57 (275)	0.99
15 FEB 1990	6:56 (91.2)	17:42 (240.1)	23:59 (102)	9:21 (232)	0.68
28 FEB 1990	6:39 (85.1)	17:56 (246.2)	8:06 (58)	22:20 (277)	0.15
10 MAR 1990	6:24 (80.1)	18:06 (251.2)	17:42 (71)	5:50 (263)	0.99
15 MAR 1990	6:16 (77.5)	18:12 (253.7)	22:48 (105)	7:50 (229)	0.83
31 MAR 1990	5:51 (69.4)	18:27 (261.8)	8:55 (40)		0.31

TIMES BELOW: MDT

Date	Sunrise (azm)	Sunset (azm)	Moonrise(azm)	Moonset(azm)	Phase
9 APR 1990	6:37 (65.0)	19:36 (266.2)	19:35 (91)	6:02 (244)	0.99
15 APR 1990	6:28 (62.2)	19:42 (269.1)	0:28 (112)	9:31 (220)	0.73
30 APR 1990	6:08 (55.6)	19:56 (275.6)	11:06 (46)	1:24 (287)	0.38
8 MAY 1990	5:59 (52.6)	20:04 (278.7)	19:29 (101)	4:55 (233)	0.99
15 MAY 1990	5:52 (50.2)	20:10 (281.1)	0:36 (105)	10:24 (228)	0.70
31 MAY 1990	5:41 (46.1)	20:23 (285.1)	13:21 (72)	1:26 (263)	0.54
7 JUN 1990	5:39 (44.9)	20:28 (286.3)	20:21 (111)	4:38 (222)	0.99
15 JUN 1990	5:38 (44.2)	20:32 (287.0)	0:33 (81)	12:38 (254)	0.54
30 JUN 1990	5:42 (44.4)	20:34 (286.7)	14:13 (91)	0:37 (244)	0.58
7 JUL 1990	5:46 (45.2)	20:33 (285.9)	20:41 (108)	5:07 (221)	0.99
15 JUL 1990	5:51 (46.7)	20:29 (284.4)		13:58 (276)	0.46
31 JUL 1990	6:04 (51.1)	20:17 (280.0)	16:04 (109)	0:32 (224)	0.70
6 AUG 1990	6:09 (53.2)	20:11 (277.8)	20:20 (93)	6:08 (234)	0.99
15 AUG 1990	6:18 (56.7)	20:00 (274.3)	0:40 (40)	16:33 (291)	0.26
31 AUG 1990	6:32 (63.8)	19:37 (267.2)	17:12 (107)	1:42 (222)	0.81
1 SEP 1990	6:33 (64.3)	19:35 (266.8)	17:48 (102)	2:45 (226)	0.88
4 SEP 1990	6:36 (65.7)	19:31 (265.3)	19:13 (81)	6:06 (245)	0.99
15 SEP 1990	6:46 (71.1)	19:13 (259.9)	3:04 (52)	17:28 (275)	0.11
30 SEP 1990	6:59 (78.6)	18:49 (252.4)	16:45 (92)	2:38 (235)	0.83
3 OCT 1990	7:02 (80.1)	18:44 (251.0)	18:05 (69)	6:03 (258)	0.99
15 OCT 1990	7:14 (86.0)	18:26 (245.1)	4:16 (72)	16:49 (256)	0.08

TIMES BELOW: MST

Date	Sunrise (azm)	Sunset (azm)	Moonrise(azm)	Moonset(azm)	Phase
31 OCT 1990	6:31 (93.2)	17:05 (237.8)	15:30 (65)	3:49 (263)	0.93
2 NOV 1990	6:33 (94.1)	17:03 (237.0)	16:38 (50)	6:19 (279)	0.99
15 NOV 1990	6:47 (99.0)	16:51 (232.1)	5:17 (98)	15:35 (231)	0.02
30 NOV 1990	7:03 (103.2)	16:43 (227.9)	15:09 (47)	5:07 (282)	0.96
1 DEC 1990	7:04 (103.4)	16:43 (227.7)	15:59 (43)	6:25 (287)	0.99
15 DEC 1990	7:16 (105.4)	16:43 (225.8)	6:10 (109)	15:26 (221)	0.01
31 DEC 1990	7:23 (105.1)	16:52 (226.1)	16:58 (44)	7:24 (288)	0.99
15 JAN 1991	7:22 (102.5)	17:06 (228.7)	7:14 (105)	17:01 (227)	0.00
29 JAN 1991	7:14 (98.2)	17:22 (233.0)	17:04 (52)	6:46 (281)	0.99
31 JAN 1991	7:12 (97.5)	17:24 (233.8)	19:30 (68)	7:54 (267)	0.96

Date	Sunrise (azm)	Sunset (azm)	Moonrise(azm)	Moonset(azm)	Phase
15 FEB 1991	6:56 (91.3)	17:42 (240.0)	7:12 (83)	19:03 (251)	0.01
28 FEB 1991	6:39 (85.2)	17:56 (246.1)	18:17 (72)	6:20 (263)	0.99
15 MAR 1991	6:16 (77.7)	18:11 (253.6)	5:39 (79)	17:54 (256)	0.00
29 MAR 1991	5:54 (70.6)	18:25 (260.7)	18:13 (84)	5:12 (251)	0.99
31 MAR 1991	5:51 (69.6)	18:27 (261.7)	20:23 (98)	6:07 (237)	0.97

TIMES BELOW: MDT

Date	Sunrise (azm)	Sunset (azm)	Moonrise(azm)	Moonset(azm)	Phase
15 APR 1991	6:28 (62.3)	19:41 (269.0)	6:33 (53)	21:17 (282)	0.01
28 APR 1991	6:11 (56.5)	19:54 (274.7)	20:13 (101)	5:37 (233)	0.99
30 APR 1991	6:08 (55.7)	19:56 (275.5)	22:14 (108)	6:48 (224)	0.96
15 MAY 1991	5:52 (50.3)	20:10 (281.0)	6:46 (42)	22:31 (289)	0.03
27 MAY 1991	5:43 (47.0)	20:20 (284.3)	20:06 (107)	4:46 (225)	0.99
31 MAY 1991	5:41 (46.1)	20:23 (285.1)	23:14 (104)	8:05 (225)	0.90
15 JUN 1991	5:38 (44.2)	20:32 (287.0)	9:14 (54)	23:28 (273)	0.15
26 JUN 1991	5:40 (44.1)	20:34 (287.0)	20:35 (108)	5:03 (222)	0.99
30 JUN 1991	5:42 (44.4)	20:34 (286.8)	22:46 (90)	8:58 (238)	0.88
15 JUL 1991	5:51 (46.6)	20:30 (284.5)	10:30 (74)	22:54 (253)	0.21
25 JUL 1991	5:59 (49.2)	20:23 (281.9)	19:52 (103)	4:50 (226)	0.99
31 JUL 1991	6:04 (51.0)	20:17 (280.0)	22:29 (64)	10:55 (264)	0.77
15 AUG 1991	6:17 (56.6)	20:00 (274.4)	12:40 (99)	22:50 (229)	0.36
24 AUG 1991	6:26 (60.5)	19:47 (270.5)	19:20 (88)	5:43 (240)	0.99
31 AUG 1991	6:32 (63.7)	19:37 (267.3)	22:55 (44)	13:15 (286)	0.60
15 SEP 1991	6:45 (71.0)	19:13 (260.1)	14:22 (109)	23:41 (222)	0.48
23 SEP 1991	6:53 (75.0)	19:01 (256.1)	18:38 (69)	6:37 (258)	0.99
30 SEP 1991	6:59 (78.5)	18:49 (252.6)	23:52 (45)	14:14 (287)	0.52
15 OCT 1991	7:14 (85.9)	18:26 (245.2)	14:20 (102)		0.50
22 OCT 1991	7:21 (89.2)	18:17 (241.9)	17:34 (58)	6:30 (270)	0.99

TIMES BELOW: MST

Date	Sunrise (azm)	Sunset (azm)	Moonrise(azm)	Moonset(azm)	Phase
31 OCT 1991	6:30 (93.1)	17:05 (237.9)	0:15 (60)	13:50 (267)	0.33
15 NOV 1991	6:47 (98.9)	16:51 (232.2)	13:11 (82)	0:04 (245)	0.61
21 NOV 1991	6:54 (100.8)	16:47 (230.3)	16:27 (45)	6:39 (285)	0.99
30 NOV 1991	7:03 (103.1)	16:43 (228.0)	1:31 (81)	13:17 (246)	0.27
15 DEC 1991	7:16 (105.3)	16:43 (225.8)	12:28 (64)	0:53 (263)	0.63
31 DEC 1991	7:23 (105.1)	16:52 (226.1)	3:43 (104)	13:30 (226)	0.15
15 JAN 1992	7:22 (102.5)	17:06 (228.7)	12:49 (45)	3:02 (284)	0.77
19 JAN 1992	7:21 (101.5)	17:10 (229.7)	17:20 (52)	7:02 (281)	0.99
31 JAN 1992	7:12 (97.6)	17:24 (233.7)	5:11 (107)	14:46 (225)	0.07
15 FEB 1992	6:57 (91.4)	17:41 (239.8)	14:52 (49)	4:49 (284)	0.90
17 FEB 1992	6:54 (90.5)	17:43 (240.7)	17:25 (63)	6:12 (272)	0.99
29 FEB 1992	6:38 (84.8)	17:57 (246.4)	4:25 (101)	14:35 (232)	0.12
15 MAR 1992	6:15 (77.3)	18:12 (254.0)	15:00 (59)	4:05 (275)	0.87

Date	Sunrise (azm)	Sunset (azm)	Moonrise(azm)	Moonset(azm)	Phase
18 MAR 1992	6:10 (75.8)	18:15 (255.5)	18:40 (83)	5:43 (252)	0.99
31 MAR 1992	5:50 (69.2)	18:28 (262.1)	4:17 (81)	16:21 (254)	0.05

TIMES BELOW: MDT

Date	Sunrise (azm)	Sunset (azm)	Moonrise(azm)	Moonset(azm)	Phase
15 APR 1992	6:27 (61.9)	19:42 (269.3)	18:29 (87)	5:11 (248)	0.97
16 APR 1992	6:26 (61.5)	19:43 (269.8)	19:40 (94)	5:43 (241)	0.99
30 APR 1992	6:07 (55.4)	19:57 (275.8)	4:35 (63)	18:13 (271)	0.04
15 MAY 1992	5:51 (50.0)	20:11 (281.2)	19:38 (102)	4:50 (231)	0.99
31 MAY 1992	5:41 (46.0)	20:24 (285.2)	4:59 (45)	20:21 (287)	0.00
14 JUN 1992	5:38 (44.2)	20:32 (287.0)	20:24 (107)	5:00 (224)	0.99
15 JUN 1992	5:38 (44.1)	20:32 (287.0)	21:11 (105)	5:54 (224)	0.99
30 JUN 1992	5:42 (44.4)	20:34 (286.7)	5:47 (46)	20:56 (283)	0.00
13 JUL 1992	5:50 (46.4)	20:30 (284.7)	19:51 (104)	4:43 (226)	0.99
15 JUL 1992	5:51 (46.8)	20:29 (284.3)	20:59 (95)	6:41 (233)	0.99
31 JUL 1992	6:05 (51.3)	20:16 (279.8)	8:24 (68)	21:20 (259)	0.05
12 AUG 1992	6:15 (55.7)	20:03 (275.3)	19:31 (92)	5:33 (236)	0.99
15 AUG 1992	6:18 (57.0)	19:59 (274.1)	20:47 (73)	8:27 (255)	0.94
31 AUG 1992	6:33 (64.1)	19:36 (267.0)	10:53 (95)	21:29 (233)	0.18

Appendix 6 • **Directory**

CENTRAL RESERVATIONS (for all huts except Diamond J Guest Ranch and Rocky Mountain Health Ranch)

10th Mountain Trail Association
1280 Ute Avenue
Aspen CO 81611
(303)925-5775

PRIVATE RESERVATIONS

Diamond J Guest Ranch
(303)927-3222

Rocky Mountain Health Ranch
(303)927-3570

Shrine Mountain Inn Restaurant
(303)476-5733

Pilgrim's Inn
(303)827-5333

SHUTTLE SERVICES
Main Mountain Rides
(303)920-0168

Trailhead Transit
(800)634-4813 (in state)
(800)621-6131 (out of state)

GUIDES
Elk Mountain Guides
(303)925-9075

Paragon Guides
(303)949-4272

CROSS COUNTRY SKI CENTERS
Ashcroft Ski Touring
(303)925-1971

Aspen Cross Country Center
(303)925-2145

Ski Cooper Nordic Center
(719)486-2277

Snowmass Club Touring Center
(303)923-3148

Vail/Beaver Creek Cross Country Ski Center
(303)476-5601 x4390

AREA INFORMATION
Vail Activities Desk
(303)949-5750

USGS MAPS
USGS
Bx 25286 Denver Federal Center
Denver CO 80225

WEATHER
(900)932-8437

AVALANCHE INFORMATION
Aspen: (303)920-1664

Denver/Boulder: (303)236-9435

Dillon: (303)468-5434

Minturn: (303)827-5687

FOREST SERVICE

Aspen Ranger District (White River National Forest)
(303)925-3445

Eagle Ranger District (White River National Forest)
(303)328-6388

Holy Cross Ranger District (White River National Forest)
(303)827-5715

Leadville Ranger District (San Isabel National Forest)
(719)486-0752

Sopris Ranger District (White River National Forest)
(303)963-2266

COUNTY SHERIFF DEPARTMENTS

Eagle County
(303)927-3244/328-6611

Lake County
(719)486-1249/486-1274

Pitkin County
(303)920-5300/963-3030

Summit County
(303)825-6328 (metro)
(303)453-6222 (local)

LOCAL STORES

Aspen

The Hub of Aspen (303)925-7970

Ute Mountaineer (303)925-2849

Carbondale

Life Cycles (303)963-1149

Glenwood Springs

Summit Canyon Mountaineering (303)945-6994

Leadville

Back of Beyond (719)486-2836

Bill's Sport Shop (719)486-0739

Vail/Avon

Christi Sports (303)949-0241

Bibliography

Barnett, Steve. *Cross Country Downhill*, 3rd ed. Seattle: Pacific Search Press, 1983.

Burton, Hale. *The Ski Troops*, New York: Simon and Schuster, 1971.

Casewit, Curtis W. *MOUNTAIN TROOPERS!*, New York: Thomas Y. Crowell Company.

Dawson, Louis W. *Colorado High Routes*, Seattle: The Mountaineers, 1986.

Kelner, Alexis and Hanscom, David. *Wasatch Tours*, Salt Lake City: Wasatch Publishers, Inc., 1976.

LaChapelle, Edward R. *The ABC of Avalanche Safety*, 2nd ed., Seattle: The Mountaineers, 1985.

Ohlrich, Warren H. *Aspen/Snowmass Cross Country Ski Trails*, Aspen: WHO Press, 1989.

Ohlrich, Warren H. *Aspen/Snowmass Guide to Outdoor Activities*, Aspen: WHO Press, 1988.

Ohlrich, Warren H. *Aspen/Snowmass Trails*, Aspen: WHO Press, 1988.

Parker, Paul. *Free-Heel Skiing*, Diadem Books: England

Peters, Ed. *Mountaineering, the Freedom of the Hills*, 4th ed., Seattle: The Mountaineers, 1982.

Perla, Ronald and Martinelli, M. *Avalanche Handbook*, Washington, D.C.: U.S. Department of Agriculture #489, 1976.

Tejada-Flores, Lito. *Backcountry Skiing*, San Francisco: Sierra Club Books, 1981.

Watters, Ron. *Ski Camping*, San Francisco: Solstice Press/Chronicle Books, 1979.

Williams, Knox and Armstrong, Betsy. *The Snowy Torrents –Avalanche Accidents in the United States 1972-1979*, Jackson, Wyoming: Teton Bookshop Publishing Company.

Williams, Knox and Armstrong, Betsy. *The Avalanche Book*, Golden, Colorado: Fulcrum, Inc., 1986.

Index

L

Lake Creek Road, 36
Larkspur Mountain, 31
Larkspur Mountain Road, 54-55
Laura's Lines, 167
Leadville, 5, 39-40, 62, 66, 149, 155, 168, 170-71, 174
Lenado, 31, 52
Lenado Alternate Trailhead, 31, 48
Lenado Gulch, 31, 41, 45, 48
Lenado Road, 31
Lenado Trailhead, 31, 46-47, 52-55
Lily Lake, 160
Lime Creek, 77, 79-80, 93-94, 113
Lime Creek Canyon, 78-79, 94
Lime Creek Road, 113-15, 132
Lime Drainage Trail, 74, 82-83, 94
Lime Park, 67, 77-82, 86, 93-94, 97
Lime Ridge, 82-83, 94
Lime Ridge Trail, 74, 81-82, 89, 93-94
Little Lime Creek, 79-83, 89, 93-95
Logged Off Mountain, 107
Longs Creek, 172-73
Longs Gulch, 163, 172-73
Longs Gulch Trail, 163
Lower Van Horn Park, 45-46, 48
Lower Van Horn Saddle, 45

M

Main Range Trail, 157, 163, 168, 170, 172, 174
Margy's Hut, 3, 34, 41, 44, 47, 49, 50, 52-61, 63, 66, 74, 176
Maroon Bells-Snowmass Wilderness, 5
McAllister Gulch, 120-22
McGinley Gulch, 99
McNamara, Margy, 41, 52
McNamara, Robert, 41, 52
McNamara Hut, 3, 19, 31, 41-52, 59-60, 176
Middle Creek, 82, 93
Middle Cunningham Creek, 70

Midway Pass, 44
Mill Creek, 37, 113-14
Mill Creek Road, 37, 113-14
Minturn, 38
Montgomery Flats, 74-76
Mosquito Range, 162, 172
Mountain Haven Trailhead, 32-34, 63, 67, 74-76
Mount Massive, 69-70, 167
Mount of the Holy Cross, 96, 109
Mount Yeckel, 52, 60-61
Muckawanago, 62
Muckawanago Creek, 62
Mushroom Bowl, 113

N

Nast Lake, 34
Newcomer Spring, 96, 99, 103, 105
Newcomer Spring Trail, 91
New England Traverse, 104
New York Mountain, 98-99, 106
Nolan Creek, 99, 103
Norrie Colony, 33
Norrie Trailhead, 32-33, 56-57, 63, 66
North Fork Road, 34, 69-70, 160
North Fork West Tennessee Creek, 156-57, 160, 162, 173
North Maroon Peak, 120

O

Overlook Point, 75-76

P

Pando, 39, 123, 140
Pando Trailhead, 38-39, 121-26, 140-41, 177
Peak 12234, 61
Pearl Creek, 120, 133-34, 140-41, 143-46, 148
Peter Estin Hut, 7, 74, 80-83, 87-97, 105, 176
Peterson, Pete, 156

T

U

V

W

Y

Z